A FATEFUL
INHERITANCE

A FATEFUL
INHERITANCE

JUDITH CONDON

Library of Congress Control Number: 2007904306
ISBN: Hardcover   978-1-4257-7524-7
                   Softcover   978-1-4257-7487-5

This book was printed in the United States of America.

To order additional copies of this book, contact:
Xlibris Corporation
1-888-795-4274
www.Xlibris.com
Orders@Xlibris.com
40065

Contents

FOREWORD

The Haunting

My candle burns at both ends
It will not last the night;
But ah, my foes, and oh, my friends –
It gives a lovely light.

– Edna St. Vincent Millay, 1892-1950

The seeds of this haunting family history took root in me back on October 15, 1981, when I happened upon a letter from an auntie sketching out the birth and death dates of several ancestors at the turn of the twentieth century. My immediate reaction to the reading was an engulfing feeling of grief. I remember thinking, why am I crying? I didn't know any of these people. They lived so long ago. Little did I know that I was beginning an adventure into what I would call my "genetic" memory – that deep core where a well of ancestral emotional experience lay unused, unresolved, and like the magma in some unidentified volcano, just awaiting the right human vehicle to spew it all forward.

And so began the haunting. Over the next twenty-five years, a certain ancestor – Ella Condon, who died tragically in 1904 – would poke at my sensitivities, niggle her way into conversations and observations, steal into my dream states, exploit my emotions, and wring from them her unresolved grief and anger.

Of course, I had no idea what had befallen me. I was in no particular distress of any kind, physical or emotional. I was a young mother and wife, with a satisfying teaching career.

I kept journals back in those days, probably more out of self-centeredness than anything else. I mean, after all, who is going to care how I felt about something or interpreted something? I remember the reaction of a young man I once knew when he inadvertently left his journal behind on the bus and lost it to the eyes of the world. You'd have thought he'd left a child behind! I mean, who really cares? That said, I have to admit that when I read back now, I realize that Ella was revealing herself to me bit by bit through the writing and her tenacious "presence."

Ella wanted her story told, for what reason I am unsure. To emote? To warn others? For justice's sake? Only she knows the real answer. Based on my experience over these many years, I have to believe that haunting occurs in order to reveal and heal the grief of the past. I am just here to tell it all to you. You, the reader, get to decide.

The William Condon Family sans Ellie

CHAPTER 1

The Inquest: Interurban No. 23

*We the jury do hereby find that deceased came to her death
by being knocked down and crushed by a streetcar on the
Waterloo, Cedar Falls and Northern Railway and we,
the jury, do not determine who is to blame. Substance of
verdict of coroner's jury to inquire into the death of
Miss Ella Condon, killed last night at Sans Souci Park.*

– *Waterloo Daily Courier*, Saturday evening, June 4, 1904

*The inquest required a room big enough to hold some 20-25 people,
the coroner, the jurymen, medical and lay witnesses, and,
occasionally representatives of relatives, the deceased,
or an insurance company . . . The body upon which the inquest
was held would also be present for jurors to view.*

– Victor Bailey, '*This Rash Act*,' Stanford Press, 1998

Two Conductors

"I'm reading it, gentlemen, but I'm not so easy with it," declared Coroner McManus to J. C. Murtagh, one of three jurors he'd selected to study the evidence collected following young Miss Condon's gruesome death. "For one thing, that car was backing up slowly, so slowly that a flea could have walked a circus across that track and not harmed a hair on anyone's head." McManus had been struggling with his jurors' decision for hours now, and his discomfort was unresolved, even though he'd no choice but to release it to the newspaper.

"What do you think, Peterson?" R. E. Peterson, still uneasy following his encounter with Miss Condon's disheveled remains, chose not to speak, sobered as he was by the mutilation. "Brinker, what say you?" repeated the coroner. "I'm just stymied, Mac. The testimony from the conductors, Dixon and Parkins, did not convince me that this was an accident; but we found no evidence to the contrary. Even that third conductor, H. T. Turner, who was walking at the back of the train, told us that this young woman did not attempt to run across the tracks. He was right there. He would have seen her if she had been that reckless."

"I will ask you again, what do you make of it?" demanded McManus. "What else can we do? We had to determine that the crowd swelled and pushed her onto the tracks," said Peterson, at last emerging from the shadows.

"Your determination as a jury said absolutely nothing to solve this case or to give this family any answers! 'We the jury does not determine who is to blame.' What kind of inquest results is that? I entrusted you to put it all together, and you went down like three stones in quicksand."

All three hung their heads in response to the coroner's indictment. Brinker was nervous. He needed to get back to his dairy cows. They were overdue for milking. Murtagh and Peterson were exhausted from the past day's events and could not put two thoughts together at this point in time.

Murtagh spoke hesitantly, "If you're not satisfied with our verdict, Mac, why did you release it to the newspeople?" McManus laid a cold eye on Murtagh. "Are you not a father? Put yourself in the place of this family, devastated by having to bury their child. I just wanted to have something that would help put their pain to rest, but this case is far from settled in my mind. You, however, are free to go back to your chores. If something jogs your memory or if there are any questions left in your minds, please come see me. I'm going to be working with this for a while."

The three jurors took caps in hand and quickly left the hotel before McManus could change his mind. McManus sat at his desk with inquest papers scattered here and there and thought what he might be doing if this were his beloved daughter who had been so tragically killed. He kept thinking about the look on William Condon's face when he came in to identify his young daughter. Mac had tried to cover most of the damage, but the father needed to see it all. *I've never seen a man so destroyed,* he thought. *I've got to play this out. This child deserves a better resolution. I've seen a lot,* he thought to himself, *but this case is haunting me; how does one return to the ordinary once faced with a myriad of horrific possibilities?*

Mac pulled out the newspaper and began to read.

Miss Ella Condon, eighteen years of age, met a horrible death under the wheels of a streetcar at Sans Souci Park at 10:15 last night. The body was wedged under the trucks so closely that it was an hour before the remains could be extricated. Miss Condon has been in the employ of E. M. Storm for the past week in the capacity of domestic, and early last evening, went to Sans Souci in company with Mrs. Storms's sister, Miss Lois Wissinger (Winninger), to spend a few hours seeking pleasure while listening to the band concert and meeting friends. But the pleasure trip ended in a tragic accident, and death in its most horrifying form proved to be hot on the trail of social diversion.

The car, which crushed out the life of the young lady, was No. 23, one of the interurbans used on the Denver line but which was installed last evening to aid in conveying the throng of people from the city to the parks and home again. It was in the charge of Motorman Dixon and Conductor Parkins. Just how the accident occurred is not exactly known, but from the evidence of the spectators, two theories might be reasonable and either might be true.

The accident occurred immediately after the last selection was played by the band and at a time when the large crowd of people dispersed and made their way in surging multitudes to the Rapid Transit Station. One theory is that the crowd, anxious to board this particular car, surged about the track and pushed Miss Condon in front of the car, which was backing slowly to its position.

Another theory is that the young lady, seeing that fewer people were on the opposite side of the track and that if she were there her chances for getting aboard would be increased, started too late to cross in front of the car and was run down.

There was a large crowd about and many eyewitnesses to the fatal accident. Miss Condon was seen to take a step almost in front of the car, voluntarily, or because she was pushed by people behind. As she was borne down, she uttered a terrible scream and in an instant, it was all over. The girl had been caught fairly under the motor case. She was badly mutilated about the head and face, her neck was broken and one leg was broken and there were several serious wounds about the body showing that death must have been instantaneous.

The car was moving very slowly, so witnesses say, about as fast as a person naturally walks, but before the alarm could be given to the motorman, the body had been drawn about fifteen feet and was probably turned over and over, because when the remains were taken out, the upper part of the body was facing downward and the remainder was facing upward.

Sans Souci Hotel, Waterloo, Iowa

The officials of the Rapid Transit line built the Sans Souci Hotel in 1898 in order to attract the resort trade. It was near the end of the Sans Souci Bridge.

HAD TO JACK UP THE CAR

The remains of Miss Condon were wedged under the motor case so tightly that it was impossible to remove them without further mutilating them until jackscrews had been secured with which to raise the heavy coach. Men were dispatched at once to the roundhouse for jacks. They were brought back as quickly as possible and put to use, but despite the energetic manner in which the railway employees worked, it was fully an hour after the accident happened before the body was taken out.

Those who aided in removing the remains were Mr. Litchford an employee of the roundhouse, J. F. Hecklinger of Cedar Falls, who runs motors 2 and 27 and others who worked as fast as they could.

The body was removed to the Sans Souci Hotel and Dr. Gollmar was called. The physician found that life had been extinct for some time and could therefore do nothing. He made only a casual examination of the remains. The body was then conveyed to this city and taken to Hanlon's undertaking parlors, where it was prepared for burial. The undertaker found that the injuries inflicted were many and very serious, the neck had been broken, the face and head had been cut and other hurts were inflicted about the body.

REMAINS IDENTIFIED

The accident created the utmost furor and excitement among the pleasure seekers at Sans Souci and when the news spread among the people that a young lady had been killed, those who had daughters or sisters were fearful lest some member of their family might be the fated one. All the time the remains were under the car trucks, it was not known definitely who the victim was. After the body had been removed, it was some little time before the young lady was identified by Miss Lois Wissinger (Winninger), who made the identification more by the clothing than by the appearance of the features. (*Waterloo Daily Courier*, Saturday evening, June 4, 1904)

Mac set the paper down and, taking out a pencil, began to circle standout phrases. "Two theories might be reasonable and either might be true." "The car was moving very slowly." "Miss Condon was seen to take a step almost in front of the car voluntarily or because she was pushed." "He made only a casual examination of the remains."

There's more here, thought Mac. *I just know it. While Miss Condon's body may not have made it to the autopsy table, by god, her case would.* He'd see to that.

Miss Ella Condon circa 1890's

CHAPTER 2

Miss Ella

Ellie A. Condon
February 17, 1886-June 3, 1904
"The Good Die Young"

– Grave inscription, Calvary Cemetery, Waterloo, Iowa

After the ball is over, after the break of morn,
After the dancers' leaving, after the stars are gone,
Many a heart is aching, if you could read them all –
Many the hopes that have vanished, after the ball.

– Charles K. Harris, Milwaukee, Wisconsin, 1892

I came in on February 17, 1886, the first girl child in an Irish American farm family. Born in DeKalb County, Illinois, we came in an open covered wagon to our farm near Waterloo, Iowa, when we were little. I believe that we all make choices before we are born, so I have no one to blame or to congratulate but myself for the life I was about to experience. I must have needed to learn some hard lessons. I hope they travel with me so I don't need to relearn them if there is a second time around!

They named me Ella, Ella Condon – a plain, conservative name for the not-so-conservative adult child I would become. Growing up at the end of one century and leaping the cusp of the next had both its joys and its challenges, but oh, what an adventure!

I don't remember much about my childhood, except that I always felt "different," not special, but "different," as though I saw and understood things no one else in my family knew. I was a keen "feeler," sensing things that entered my arena. I couldn't explain how I knew things, I just did.

My family wasn't wealthy, but we were lucky to have the farm and all that went with it. We worked that farm in Bennington Township, seven miles from Waterloo, a river and railroad community. Mother and Da were first generation Americans, children of Irish immigrants who fled famine and certain death in Ireland. Some might call that good fortune, to get out of there. Me? I felt trapped between a joy and melancholia I could not name but observed and felt every day of my life.

As in most Irish families of the time, Mother let Da believe that he ruled the roost, but he'd have been lost without her. The Irish are a matriarchal society, no matter what they say, with a long history of pagan goddesses and Celtic warrior queens to back us up. Da's father came to the States from the west of Ireland. No one ever spoke of why he left, but we knew from studying history that the recent famines had all but decimated Ireland's population. My grandpa, James Condon – born in Tipperary, Ireland, in May of 1820 – came out of the port of Cork on June 3, 1848, probably on one of those famine ships. This one was called the Jane Anderson. Grandpa was listed as a "laborer."

Lucky, I thought, that Grandpa got through when he did. The neighbors still talked about the number of Irish who had died in America's Civil War. Though they had fled certain death in Ireland from the famines, plague, and poverty, it seemed ironic to me that so many were conscripted right off the boats by wily rogues promising food and wages. From the coffin ships straight into the arms of the American military, there was just no accounting for justice here or anywhere else.

I don't know where he met my grandma, Catherine Walsh, because she was born in County Mayo, Ireland, on June 26, 1825. Both of them are buried back in St. Mary's Cemetery, DeKalb, Illinois. Grandpa died on October 6, 1900, and Grandma, March 28, 1911. They had been married in Milwaukee, Wisconsin, in 1848 at Sts. John and Peter Catholic Church; and Da was born in Milwaukee. Grandpa moved them all to DeKalb County to farm when Da was an infant. That is where my da and ma met. She was from Rockford, Illinois. Once Da and Ma moved from DeKalb, we rarely saw the grandparents again. I always missed them. Now, I wish I'd had asked more questions of them.

Emigrating from Ireland must have been a prodigious decision, yet rare was the moment of explanation. While there was inherent pride in being Irish, there was also a kind of unspoken shame and sadness at leaving the homeland. The reticence of my grandparents to reveal their pain and loss left me with the conclusion that perhaps unresolved grief passes on from one generation to the next. Perhaps my brother Jimmy's melancholia wasn't really his at all.

The Irish are full of mystery, rarely giving away much of themselves. From the time we learn to talk, we know to always answer a question with a question, never a direct answer. After all, one must discern to whom one is speaking. If I have heard it once, I have heard it a thousand times, "Don't be airing your dirty laundry now!" We Irish keep things close to the heart, but those things often spill up into our eyes, and we have to be carefully stoic or people may surmise too much.

My life would be a short one by most people's standards, eighteen years, but it would take me much longer to tell my story. My day of reckoning would come on June 3, 1904, much to my surprise. You see, we "feelers" pick up lots of information about others, but rarely do we recognize the clues to our own. Or do we? After all, we are all connected in this web called life. Perhaps, I should have paid closer attention. Perhaps if I had, "it" would not have happened. Oh, but I'm getting ahead of myself.

I have several brothers – Bernie, Carl, Will, Jack, Len, and James – and a little sister, Elsie. I was born between James and Jack. Most of us are a little more than one year apart. Ma was a busy woman, changing and feeding the young ones, cooking for the hired men, canning, collecting the eggs, slopping the pigs, no wonder she never looked very happy.

As I said, the Irish are a funny lot, living somewhere between joy and melancholia every day of their lives. They are either dancing and singing or wailing their grief. There is not a lot of in-between, more hills and valleys, which make me wonder why we settled out here in the Midwestern plains. Maybe Da was looking for balance.

Da purchased the Stubbs farm in 1890, with 160 acres of rich, dark earth. I love the smell that rises from the tilled dirt when the spring rains hammer down. It's an old, familiar smell, ancient, really, with roots that go down into my very soul. The house sits upon the highest hill in the county overlooking a barn, granary, chicken coop, machine shed, smokehouse, and several other smaller functional buildings, including the stinky outhouse. I'd rather do almost anything than empty the chamber pots or have to have a sit down out there!

My favorite buildings on the farm are the barn and the "crazy house," a nearly destroyed old granary that has been caught in one too many windstorms, it leans to its side and sends me spinning as I enter and try to stand up inside. I spend hours with little Elsie in the barn's hayloft creating scenarios for her dolls. We have to be careful not to step in a hole and end up in the cow manure down below. Cows are curious animals, wondering what we odd creatures are up to just above their massive heads.

My brothers do all of the milking. I love it when they turn a teat and squirt milk out to the feral kittens who nearly overrun this farm. Have you ever seen a kitten drool? The piglets are the sweetest, softest little creatures. They squeal and slip this way and that, trying to follow their mothers to the morsels from the slop bucket we bring down from the house twice a day.

There is so much beauty on our farm, from the apple orchard to groves to pastures, but the most beautiful part is the timelessness of it all. The earth is ageless. If I could come back here in one hundred years, the dark earth would smell exactly the same after a spring downpour, fresh like wind and water sprinkled with roses. The pasture behind the grove and next to the apple orchard overlooks a vast expanse of farmland. It's my private space. I go there to be alone, to sing and dance under huge milky clouds blown this way and that by an invisible wizard with powerful breath. I love the endless, dusty golden cornfields and the thunderstorms with their powerful sky partners, bolts of cracking light, shaking the earth and air, drenching my rawboned shoulders with cold pellets of rolling energy.

Sometimes I search for treasures long forgotten under layers of history, arrowheads from a lost tribe, the bones of small animals, a purple blossom stretching its neck out of and through old cornstalks – signs of life and a passion to go on and on. I wonder how many of us walk unawares over treasures every day. I have discovered that if I listen carefully, I can almost hear them cry out to be discovered.

I remember the day the gravestone revealed itself to me. How many times had I passed by that gray slab in the earth at the back of the house? Countless numbers, but one day, it called out to me for attention. I stooped down and began to dig with my bare hands into the small knoll of grass and weeds. It was a struggle, but at last it came free; and I overturned it to discover the gravestone of a baby, long dead. When I questioned Ma, she told me that she and Da had removed it from its spot in the front yard where the child was buried. I remember the shock I felt knowing that I had been playing ball with my brothers, running atop her resting place, ignorant of her presence entirely. If we were not remembering her, who would? Do the dead just disappear once time piles upon them the minutiae of everyday life?

Some mysteries – Mother said – are best left buried. I thought about that for a long time, and every night when I went to bed, that little baby's spirit went with me. I just could not help but wonder what calamity had befallen her. Was it any coincidence that we lived on top of her? What was she teaching me with her haunting memory?

If I had known what calamities were going to befall us, I think I would have paid more attention to that baby's spirit. Looking back now, I find it so odd that Elsie and I, the only daughters in a ponderous mass of brothers, would both die so young and so tragically. The brothers faired slightly better, all except James, that is. He and I had a special bond; perhaps that is why he made the devastating choice he made. I have often wondered how grown-ups make choices. How do they know what the right answers are? Is there a book somewhere that guides them? Or do they only make the important decisions when they are desperate and must do something?

No one goes through life unscathed, but some are far more scathed than others are. The very nature of rural life in the last decade of the nineteenth century promoted isolation. Transportation was horse and buggy, and it took a long time to get anywhere. The city was a full seven miles from our home, so playmates were hard to come by. The brothers and the occasional visit from the city cousins were my main source of entertainment. What would I have done without Jimmy? James and I were close; he was born the year before I came in, though in most Irish Catholic families, there is not a lot of space between the children. Most people around here refer to a nine-month span as "Irish twins." My older brothers are typical of the Irish male. Most are shy with women. They will all live at home until each has the courage to step out and court a young woman and then ask for her hand in marriage. The exception in our family is my younger brother, Wilbur. He's the funny one. Girls love his sense of humor. Only sixteen years old, he makes them laugh. He wants desperately to walk out with Mary Kane, a tiny redhead and the oldest of ten children from Fairbanks; but at twelve, she is still too young. I think Will loves her. He goes all moony-faced if I bring up her name.

Jimmy is another story all together. He's more sensitive than the other boys, more generous of spirit, putting others' needs before his own. He is also the odd one in our family, the only light-haired child. We, the rest of us, are what people call "dark Irish," but we all have the blue eyes. Jimmy is nearly blond, no doubt due to some throwback ancestor who wrecked off the Irish coast. I spend more time with Jimmy than the others. We both love to wander around the pastures – me singing and dancing for the cows, and he hunting small game animals. One day my parents would report that Jimmy was killed in a "hunting accident." It would be one of the great lies of this family. James and I knew better, but by then, we'd both be gone.

Trolley Car

CHAPTER 3

The Inquest

*Coroners, especially urban ones, seem to have held inquests
on most of the unnatural, sudden or suspicious deaths
reported to them.*

– Victor Bailey, 'This Rash Act'

McManus mused over the news account of Miss Condon's death. *Questions and more questions,* he thought. *Why were there more people at this concert than ever before this? Why did she desire to be there? Was she, perhaps, meeting someone? More importantly, why was she hired on as a domestic when her parents were obviously successful farmers? Why does an Irish girl leave her parents' home prior to marriage? Why all of the emphasis on her being such a "good girl"?* It just didn't add up. There was more to this story, and someone knew it, someone besides the deceased.

McManus knew he would have to interview the family members. He dreaded that task. How could he accomplish this without revealing to them his dissatisfaction with the outcome of the inquest? Besides, they were all so vulnerable right now. Where to start? A brother, perhaps. Leave the parents to their grieving; he might get more information from a sibling. He made a note in his calendar to learn more about the Condon family, how long they'd been in the county, where they'd originated. He'd go over to the county records office and to the church to see if there were any clues in the documents they kept. In the meantime, he would seek out Ella's brothers, starting with the three who were closest in age – Jack, Wilbur, and James.

Wilbur was nearly sixteen, James nineteen, and Jack seventeen. *I wonder how well they knew their sister,* he mused. Being of Irish descent himself, Mac knew that secrets were paramount in clannish people. The Irish, especially, were not wont to reveal too much of their private lives to others outside of the circle. That particular quirk was handed down from the days in Ireland when a native never knew for sure if he was talking with another native or to a spy from England. The Irish always got their information by answering a question with another. Mac knew he ran the risk of getting caught up into that circle of queries, but he had little choice. He needed information. He would begin with young Wilbur. He remembered someone mentioning that Will had an evening job at the railroad yard, so it wouldn't be difficult to make a captive audience of him away from the others. Mac saddled his horse and headed over to the railroad station.

Chapman Lumber Company

Trotting along, he pondered, wondering to himself if this new century – the one they'd all looked forward to and celebrated with fireworks and hoopla, a new millennium – would be the age of discovery or the age of more danger and complication. People were just beginning to settle in to the new century, and already he'd seen enough death by "accident" to fill his craw for a long time. *We need something else to help us prove that these deaths weren't all accidental, but how does one do that? Will there be any discoveries down the road that will help us both prove and disprove our theories of how people died?*

Why, the horseless streetcars had just been introduced and lauded as the answer to transportation woes in 1896; and already here I am, investigating a grisly impact of progress. The Cass family had instigated the trolley system in Waterloo. Calling it the Waterloo Cedar Falls and Northern Transit Company, they sought to carry people to recreation sites throughout the city and to haul them to work in the factories and the mills.

Mac enjoyed the rare trips he made over to the Illinois Central Railroad Yard. He remembered last June 2, when President Teddy Roosevelt had made a ten-minute "whistle-stop" speech from the train platform to the crowd surrounding him. *That Teddy was larger than life,* thought Mac, *and to think that he made a stop in our town.* Of course, Waterloo was known as a rich agricultural region, the center of farming and dairying and the place to go to purchase farm implements.

As he strolled past Chapman's Lumber Co., Mac caught the scent of Rath Packing Company and thought to himself, *Well, except for the smell, there's a good outcome of progress.* Rath Meat Packing Plant had come to Waterloo in 1891 lured by three railroads, farm productivity, and the availability of a winter labor force. The population at the time was 6,674 people, but it had brought more folks into the area. *Now we are nearing fourteen thousand citizens,* thought Mac. That was both bad and good, as the Waterloo City Police Department, a group of four men in 1894, was forced to grow as the demand for criminal investigation and prevention increased with the population. Patrols were mostly concerned with reducing alcohol consumption and preventing transients from camping in the shantytown along the river. *Why not,* thought McManus, *leave the transients and the drunks alone and become a real investigative force looking into unsolved mysteries like the one he was trying to solve on his own?*

Mac never visited the ICRR (Illinois Central Railroad Roundhouse) without being duly impressed. The ICRR, where locomotives were brought for upkeep, was a formidable building. It housed several shops: the Hose House, Handcar Shop, Lumber Sheds 1 and 2, the Bolt House, the Water Tanks, and the Oil House. An immense maintenance shed called the Back Shop was filled with stalls equipped with all the tools needed to strip and rebuild a massive steam locomotive, including hoists, which could lift over a hundred tons.

After casually sniffing around, he found Will Condon mending mailbags in the station house. Will recognized McManus as the latter entered the room. "Mr. McManus," greeted Will with surprise and a look of pained defeat. "What can I do for you?" Will was at once anxious and wary of this encounter with the coroner. "Is there something left undone with my sister?" asked Will sincerely. *The questions, already,* thought Mac. "Ah no, Will, I just need to finish up some paperwork and thought I'd have a chat with you rather than trouble your parents in their grief. "Right, sir," replied Will, looking away and back to his chore.

McManus settled himself in a wooden chair near Will's workstation and began his task. "Tell me about your sister, son. What was she like?" Will was immediately suspicious and could not for the life of him understand what these questions had to do with his sister's accident, but being polite, he picked up the thread and began to weave it with his own queries. "And sir, why would you be needing to know about my sister's ways? Will this bring her back to us?"

"Will, you and I both know the answer to that," said Mac. "I am the county coroner. Often, I only know of the person what I see in death. What truly animated them is gone. I've only the shell in which they carried themselves around to learn from, and sometimes, it is not enough. The circumstances of your sister's death were inconclusive. I've no wish to trouble your parents, but I need to know more about her to delve deeper into the mystery surrounding her death. Are you going to help me or not?"

Will, seeming to be duly chastised and near tears, nodded slowly and never looked up from his task. "Good man, shall we begin with a description of your sister's personality, her likes and dislikes, things along those lines?" And so began the grilling of Wilbur Condon. Drawing information of this sort from a nearly sixteen-year-old boy was an exercise in futility. Did they ever pay any attention to their sisters, except maybe to antagonize them? Mac had children of his own, and his boys rarely opened their mouths during their adolescence. He'd no idea what they were thinking from one moment to the next. The girls, on the other hand, all chatty, they were. Too bad Miss Ella didn't have older sisters. He'd venture that he'd have learned something from that kind of encounter.

McManus spent the better part of two hours with young Will Condon and was more intrigued than ever. Ella's younger brother had loved her very much, but it was starkly obvious to Mac that it was the older brother, James, who figured most in this young woman's life. He would be the nut to crack, and it must be accomplished sooner rather than later. Young Will had revealed more in his reticence than in all the verbiage he might have expelled, for the only family member he left out of his narratives was James.

Mac thanked Will Condon and, praising him for his efforts and wishing him good night, left the station house to look for Jack Condon, who had just begun working as a switchman for the Illinois Central Railroad. Will had mentioned that his brother was on duty tonight should Mac wish to speak with him.

McManus strode up and down the tracks in the June twilight. He loved summer evenings. They seemed to go on forever, shunning the dark and only yielding their grasp on daylight when the fireflies emerged. He'd better find Jack soon, or he would have to wait until tomorrow. Mac much preferred seeing him tonight. It was his experience that people were more vulnerable at night, some throwback to ancient days when there was no fire, no beacon to illuminate all of the beasties that prowled the dark edges of day's end.

Jack Condon – yet another version of Miss Ella herself, though a strong masculine rendition – came striding down the tracks directly in front of Mac. "Jack Condon, I presume," remarked McManus. "There you have it, sir," replied Jack. "What can I do for you?" Jack had not recognized the coroner. Mac introduced himself much the way he did with Will and asked for an interview. Unlike the younger brother, Jack Condon was immediately accommodating. Leading Mac into a small switchman's shack, he pulled over a stool and invited him to be seated.

"Jack, I've come here to learn more about your sister, Ella, her habits and the like, in hopes that I might be able to put to rest the inquest into her tragic death." "Ellie," said Jack, "we called her Ellie. She was just a year older than I. I'm afraid I gave her an awful dose of teasing, all in fun, you know; but now, if I'd known, I might have been a bit easier on her. She was such a good sport. She didn't have a mean bone in her body, always looking out for the others. Ma's destroyed, you know."

"Yes, Jack, how could she be otherwise? Ella must have been a big help to your mother. Tell me, why did Miss Ella move into Waterloo? Was she unhappy on the farm? Didn't your mother need her help with the house, cooking, chores, and the like?" As quickly as the floodgates opened, they slammed shut again. Jack's eyes shifted to a point faraway from the railroad yard then back again. Focusing upon his hands, he began to fidget with his gloves. *Damn*, thought McManus, *too many questions too quickly*.

Mac leaned forward sympathetically, "Jack?" "I'm sorry, sir. My sister's reasons for moving into town were her own. I can't speak for her, nor would I dishonor her memory by attempting to do so. If you'll excuse me now, I have to get back to work. There's a train due through here in a few minutes." And with that, Jack rose and left the shack, banging out the door in a panic.

Mac rose quickly and followed him out the door, calling, "Jack, just one last question, please?" Jack slowed but did not turn around. "Did your sister appear to be depressed, unfocused, and faraway like?" McManus held his breath hoping desperately for an answer. "Sometimes," mumbled Jack, "more so over the past month or so. That's all I have to say." And he was off.

The OK Café & Restaurant

CHAPTER 4

Seeking Pleasure at Sans Souci

Rapid Transit officials state that they hauled more people to Sans Souci last evening than they have ever hauled before to a band concert.

– Waterloo Daily Courier, Saturday evening, June 4, 1904

I finally talked Lois into going to Sans Souci tonight for the band concert. She's not one to get out of the house very much, but she loves music and I need to have a companion. The city expects a crowd, so it should not be hard to wander away from Lois as she stops to talk with people she knows.

Now, what to wear? I will want to look my best. After all, I am a city girl now and I must dress smart.

Ella laid out a black skirt, white blouse, and her boater. The weather was quite warm, but no lady was seen anywhere in public without her bonnet. She would lace her corset loosely to allow room for the panting that always came with the heat this time of year. At least they would be next to the river, and a passing breeze might find them.

Lois was older than Ella and nearly what folks would refer to as an "old maid." She had no young man courting her or ever had as far as Ella knew. Of course, she'd only just met her this week; and Lois lived down the street from her brother's family, so Ella had only seen her once or twice. Young ladies were required to have companions when they went out of their homes. It would not be proper to be seen alone in a public place. Mr. Storm arranged it so that both young ladies would go together to the park for the evening's festivities.

Ella balked at this. Her independent streak railed against anything that might be construed as a "rule." Ever the rebel, Ella had stood her ground many times in her childhood and paid the consequences for doing so. She remembered sitting at Ma's table refusing to eat the meal placed in front of her. Mammy told her, "Child, you will sit there until bedtime if you do not eat that food!" And so she sat watching the meat congeal on the plate, observing all of the chaos in the kitchen as her brothers ran in and out, making faces at her, daring her to laugh out loud. But Ella could be stoic when she needed to be, and she needed to be stoic right now; for if she'd laughed, Mammy would have had her head.

She rarely raised that stubbornness to Da. She adored him. While Ma was the disciplinarian in the family, Da had never raised a hand to her. All he had to do to bring his eldest daughter to tears was to look at her with disappointment in his eyes. It tore her apart and sent her into waves of remorse. This drove Ma crazy, of course, as no amount of spanking could tease a tear from this child's eyes.

Even the night she sat stoically at the table establishing her wee hunger strike, Da kept finding reasons to come into the kitchen to check on her and wink at her mischievously. She remembered him stoking the fire, striding past her and out to the mudroom to check on something and giving her a nudge here and there. If Ma had caught him, she would have come unglued. Maybe that's why she and Da were close, they were so alike.

Ella's heart ached at the thought of her father. It had been so hard for him to let her come to the city to work as a domestic. She had begged. Ma would hear nothing of it, but Da understood her. There wasn't much that had been denied her in her short life, but then, she didn't ask for much. Da had worked his magic on Ma, and here she was living in the city.

Ella washed up and prepared to dress for the evening. She could hear Mr. and Mrs. Storm stirring around in their parlor. They did not seem a happy pair, not like Da and Ma. Their relationship floundered somewhere between argument and stony silence. The tension in the house could be formidable, especially for a young girl who was so spontaneous. Ella had to anticipate the reaction of these folks to her every sound and move. But tonight none of that mattered. She must get to the park. Lois would be here soon.

Ella finished dressing and came slowly down the stairs, listening for clues to the mood in the house. Lois greeted her as she entered the parlor. "Ready, Ellie?" The girls took their instructions from the Storms before heading out the door, though Lois was the only one listening. Once again, rules just weren't in Ella's arena of attention.

The girls strode the several blocks to the trolley stand and waited for their ride to Sans Souci. Ella loved to ride the trolley cars. They were a fascination for her. Coming from the farm made every discovery in town a wonder. But she wasn't really thinking about that now. She had bigger things to occupy her mind, and these kept her silent for most of the short trip to the park.

"Where are you, Ellie?" declared Lois. "You seem miles away." Lois had seen Ellie only twice before this evening, and she had sensed that something was on her mind. *Maybe it's just the mixed feelings about leaving home,* thought Lois. *At any rate, the concert should be a good distraction.* "Oh, I'm just wondering if I will see anyone I know this evening," replied Ellie.

They arrived at the entrance to Sans Souci Park in the midst of a horde of people all dressed in their best and chatting animatedly with one another. Ella jumped off the trolley even before it stopped and began to search through the crowd. "Wait, Ellie," cried Misss Winninger, but Ella was lost in thought and bodies and could no longer hear her companion.

The gazebo where the band was setting up was situated between the Sans Souci Hotel and the edge of the Cedar River. Ella made her way to the latter, sweeping her hat off, unlacing her shoes; and letting her long hair down, she began to run barefoot along the river's edge. Keeping her eye out for intruders, she found a deserted spot well shaded from prying eyes and sat in the tall grass overlooking the water. Anticipating evening insects, she'd worn no scent and brought a fan along with her. *Wild child, Ma would be calling me if she could see me now.* Ella was content to sit back and allow her thoughts to engulf her.

Threads of music began to weave themselves through the air to her hiding place. She allowed them to carry her far away from Waterloo, but not so far away that she could not sense that she was no longer alone. For her true companion, the one she'd come to see, was standing tall, gazing down at the wild faerie girl in the grass.

CHAPTER 5

The Funeral

Sunday, June 5, 1904, 2:30 p.m., St. Joseph's Catholic Church, Waterloo, Iowa

The funeral of Miss Condon will be held at 2:30 tomorrow
afternoon from St. Joseph's Catholic Church and the remains
will lie in state at the Hanlon undertaking parlors until
the hour of the funeral where the friends may visit them.

– Waterloo Daily Courier, Saturday evening, June 4, 1904

The white casket in which all that was mortal of Miss Condon
lay encased was covered with a wealth of white blossoms,
emblematic of the purity of life of the deceased.

– Waterloo Daily Courier, Monday evening, June 6, 1904

No matter what one suffers, no matter what hell is loosed upon us or how long we lie awake stunned into silence by the horror of a daughter's tragedy, no matter it all, morning still comes round, birds still sing, the rooster crows, the cows bellow to be milked, chickens peck and scratch and lay, and all the world goes on as though nothing more than a hangnail occurred.

Mary Condon dragged her weary matron's body from the bed. Only forty-five years old, she was about to bury her child. This wasn't supposed to happen, not here in America, where food was plenty and life was full to overflowing with good health. Mary remembered her da and mammy whispering about the famine days in Ireland before they set their sights on America. Her mother's dearest wish was that she never had to bury a child the way they did over and over again in the famine days when children died in parents' arms, alongside pathways or shored up in cottages by fathers who could not face the shame of being unable to provide for them.

No one expected tragedy here in America, but tragedies occurred nonetheless. *Like the tenement fires in New York City or the occasional farm accident, but not here, not to me and mine,* thought Mary wearily. She slumped to her knees, head engulfed in her pillow, and wailed into the bedclothes so as not to wake little Elsie, sleeping on her pallet at the foot of the bed.

Justice and love, love and justice, bed partners to be sure, both Creator-wrought values from what the priests and nuns call a loving God, but where is God now? Where is the justice in the death of my child? Where does the love go now that the child is gone? If you were going to wrest her from me, why not take the love as well, beastly God? Mary recalled the lessons from the nuns about God not making us suffer but helping us to suffer. Well, she'd enough of suffering. If she could join her child without fear of everlasting damnation, she would do it. *But you, God, in your smug heaven, you do so enjoy our travail, do you not?*

Mary remembered her mother's whisperings with the neighbors about the lessons from the nuns and priests back in Ireland. They had their fill of all things while the people starved to death. *Are you like your dear, devoted brides and sons of the church then, God? Do you hold yourself up to look down upon us and "help" us suffer?* Mary felt a small hand on her shoulder. Elsie slid under her mother's arm and onto her lap. "Mammy?" the child queried. Mary ground the little girl into her ample bosom, all the time thinking, *You won't get this one, not in my lifetime, you won't.* Little did she know.

William and the boys had been out doing the morning chores and were heading back in to get ready for Sunday mass. *What would they think if they knew what was in my head,* thought Mary. Gratefully, William's brother and his wife would welcome them into their home following morning mass for a rest before the afternoon funeral. Mary couldn't think of eating or sleeping, but she knew that the funeral would be a large one and that she must prepare herself for all of the sympathy, the simpering bottomless vat of sympathy.

Mary dressed Elsie and herself in their blacks. *How absurd Elsie looks. What little girl wears mourning on a beautiful summer day?* Even through her clouded grief, Mary had to admit that the beauty of this particular spring and summer had been bountiful. Just last month, she'd filled the tiny farmhouse with armloads of Ellie's favorite flowers, lilacs. Their heady scent dispelled all of the pig and dairy ambience. Ellie used to say that she hoped to die in May so she could be buried up to her neck in lilacs. *Sorry, love,* thought Mary, *the lilacs have gone the way of you and your lovely broken neck, shriveled and dead, sloughing off their beauty and fragrance.*

Since no one could eat before the communion, all Mary had to do now was sit and wait while the others washed and dressed. Her mind wandered through the many doors of Ellie's childhood. *Such an odd child,* thought Mary, *often brooding, always singing or reading, dancing or writing. Like me,* she thought, *Ellie lived in the hills and valleys, never on the plains, no even keels for Ellie. This child was a throwback to Ireland, more Irish than the Irish, an American child with a romantic's heart. She'd spent hours alone in the fields, daydreaming. My Ellie, the romantic child who would never know romance, never know the touch of a man on her soft skin, the giddy whisper in her ear, the deep-down tingle in her soft places. Bah, no justice there, grim God,* thought Mary.

At 7:00 a.m., the family piled into their carriage pulled by Dandy and Old Mol, the draft horses. It was a beautiful June morning, but no one could feel the sun through the chill of choking grief. The ride to town was interminable. No one spoke a word. Slipping into the church late and leaving immediately following communion, the family chose not to speak and went immediately to the relatives to wait until the funeral time.

Condon Family Coat of Arms

CHAPTER 6

Ella

*It is in our idleness, in our dreams, that the submerged
truth sometimes comes to the top.*

– Virginia Woolf, 1882-1941

Ellie plopped down in the dusty yard and watched as the rooster made his cocky way across the outer barnyard toward his prey in the henhouse. A lifetime farm girl, she knew his intentions. Life on a farm in rural Iowa could be tedious even with the changing seasons and never-ending chores. One is challenged to find outlets for creativity. Children learned early to entertain themselves during the short spans of free time they were allotted. They sought adventure, wide-open spaces, and sometimes, even dangerous pursuits. Ma was always sending Ellie to check the water tank when she couldn't find young Carl or Elsie. She was afraid of drowning. None of the children could swim, nor could Da or Ma, another throwback to Ireland. *What strange ancestors we had,* mused Ella, *to believe it was an insult to the sea to learn how to swim! They honestly believed that if the sea wanted to take you, you must not fight it!*

Living high on a hill in Black Hawk County afforded Ellie miles of inspiration during lazy afternoons when the chores were done, and it was too hot to stay in the house. She loved to muse and write. "There's a poet buried deep inside those of us whose roots go back to Ireland," she wrote. "It must have something to do with the endless rain, the long hours of trying to fish food out of the wild waters of the Atlantic, or the near futility of farming stubborn rocky ground." Ellie had a gift for writing, her teacher at the county schoolhouse always used her work as an example for the others. Her brothers just moaned every time Ma or Da told them to work harder like their sister.

She remembered her grandmother describing the wild western coast of Ireland with its six hundred-foot cliffs, crashing waves, and endless ocean. Ellie had once inquired, "Grandma, how did you live with all of that beauty?" "Beauty," replied the grandmother, "what beauty? It was just water for miles and miles!" *It seems we all take for granted what is right in front of us,* thought Ellie.

Ellie recalled the day she found a red petticoat in Grandmother's trunk. It was another lazy summer afternoon when the high humidity had slowed everything to a crawl. She'd tossed it on and paraded down the steps and into her grandparents' parlor. Grandma had remarked how like her great-grandmother she looked and then proceeded to tell the tale of the petticoat, the very garment her mother had worn under her long black woolen skirt, the uniform of the island women who spent long hours on the strand gathering seaweed for soup and for fertilizing the barren soil of the West. *And that is about all I ever learned about my roots,* thought Ellie. Life on the farm was never about the past, but only lived in the present moment, no time for musings, only for providing sustenance and protection from the elements. On the farm, you lived and died on your stomach.

Emigrants leaving Cork

Ellie loved to cook. Her mother was never thrilled with it, but then, not much thrilled Mammy. Farm children ate the basics, meat and potatoes or "badaydas," as the aunties called them. Funny now to understand that the "pratie," or potato, Ireland's staple, was native not to Ireland but to America. Ellie remembered her grandmother fondly. Her ma's mother, she lived nearer to the town; and when she was little, Ellie often spent an overnight with her. She recalled Grandma Curran's kitchen, more the lower half of her kitchen. Ellie had spent hours sitting under her grandma's white-painted wooden kitchen table with its small drawer full of kitchen treasures splayed out before her. Grandma's kitchen always smelled warm and yeasty. She recalled how her grandmother made her "white" coffee with cream and sugar and served it to her in her squatter's space along with warm fresh bread swathed in butter and jelly. She remembered the sticky feeling of oozy blackberry jam running down her baby chin. The sun that poured in the high windows had made shadowy puppets on the floor as she manipulated the drawer's utile trinkets.

Ellie's reverie was interrupted by her brother, Jimmy, as he ambled in from his chores, shuffling pig manure from his boots and wishing he were anywhere but here in this godforsaken dust bowl of a farm. Spitting the grit from his throat, he waved at Ellie and yelled, "Supper ready?" as he headed for the pump and a cool drink of water. "Ask Ma," replied Ellie, too lazy to move to an upright position.

James sauntered into the smokehouse and poked around for a bit of jerky from Ma's last batch. He was desperately hungry and more than a little bit disgruntled, but chewing on the jerky would give him some small comfort.

Hunger comes from such a primal space, thought Ella, *as she watched her brother forage. The will to survive, to love and be loved, to be completely and totally filled up, does anyone ever live long enough to be fully satisfied? Or are the empty spaces the key to being human? Maybe that's why we aren't perfect,* thought Ellie. *Maybe we were never meant to be. If we were perfect, we'd never need each other. I think the priests and nuns got it wrong. Even Jesus kept company with the imperfect. They were the ones who needed him.*

Mother gets nervous when I think this way, Ellie mused. *She thinks I'm a bit "odd." If only she knew about my visions. It would frighten her to death, like it used to do to me.* Ellie had become accustomed to knowing, hearing, and feeling things that she could not explain. How does one explain the feeling of impending doom, a vision of something past or future, a sense of presence disembodied? *If I gave voice to any of this,* she thought, *I might find myself living in what the folks refer to as "the funny farm." Jimmy's the only one who knows. He doesn't understand it anymore than I do, but he accepts it and calls it my "gift." The priests say that your gifts are also your crosses. If they only knew how much of a cross this gift is.*

Jimmy has the "gift" too, thought Ellie, *but he's quieter about it, shy, almost backward socially, more like a sister than a brother.* Jimmy preferred indoor tasks like cooking and baking over the outdoor chores he was charged to complete. Later he would help Ellie by collecting the lard from the fat jar in the smokehouse. It was full of the leavings from meat cooked over the past week and would make excellent piecrusts.

Ellie rolled over in the grass and breathed in the smell of sweet clover. The delicate design of this little plant belied the strength of its fragrance to grasp one's attention and send it into a dreamlike state. *Mother says I am too smart for my own good and that I daydream way too much. What else have I to do beyond school and chores? Besides, when one "knows" things, one must ponder them. Sometimes they call for action.*

In love as she was with the heady fragrances of clover and lilac, one of Ellie's least favorite things about the farm was its other pungent odors, emanating from swine and fowl dung; but sweet clover and smoking ham more than made up for it. Jimmy, too, had his own ornery way of piquing her sense of smell when he grabbed and rubbed up against her after wrestling in the pigsty. Nothing made her angrier, and he knew it. Even on the special occasions when she was allowed to ride into town, she could not escape the aura of swine, as Rath Packing Company did its best to permeate every corner of Waterloo. *It just stinks to high heaven!*

Coming to a standing position, Ellie strolled over to the barn and in to pet Buddy, the horse. She stroked his soft nose and nuzzled him with her face. The horse responded in kind to her gentle attention. Though Ellie knew that Ma would be calling supper soon, still she pulled on Buddy's saddle and mounted him. They trotted out of the barn, and Ellie lost herself in the sensual clacking sound of the horse's hooves. "Let's go, Buddy." And off they flew, Ellie was waving as she passed by Jimmy chewing on his jerky and poking a stick at Barney, the puppy. Jim's reverie was soon interrupted by Ma calling everyone to supper. Ellie was already out of ear range, the wind blowing through her coarse black mane, she'd become one with the horse.

"Where are those children?" Ma was getting impatient. Elsie was the only one at the table. She was playing with a rag doll that Ellie had made when she was born. "You try to do things right and have things nice," muttered Ma under her breath, "but do they appreciate my efforts?" Ma had a way of finding the negative in everything. Though she might have been playing with her youngest while she waited, she chose instead to stew over perceived wrongs done her.

Ma was closing in on forty-five and feeling her losses. The girl was gone, replaced by a sad woman who mostly went through the day's motions without much thought. The boys certainly took no notice. Well, maybe Jimmy, he was more like Ma – more sensitive, a sad reflection of her. She sat musing as Elsie tossed her doll up and down then squealed when Jim entered the kitchen.

"Need help, Ma?" he said. *James was a study,* thought Ma, *my only light-haired child. Where did you come from?* she thought. His brothers are so male, so oblivious to anything but their own interests; but Jimmy, so different. Ma had a hard time putting her finger on what it was that set him so apart from the rest of her brood. But that's a thought for another day. It's time to get the food on the table.

CHAPTER 7

The Funeral

Sunday afternoon, 2:30 p.m., St. Joseph's Catholic Church

Two aged ladies, bent with years, wept on each other's shoulder,
and a little grandson tugged on their skirts and said, in pained tones,
"She didn't look so pretty as she used to, but I love her just the same."

– *Waterloo Daily Courier,* June 6, 1904

The Condon family, looking world weary and near complete shutdown, walked as a unit up to the open casket at Hanlon's Undertaking Parlor. Gazing down into the casket, they were faced with the irony of Ellie's shattered countenance amid the virginal white cocoon. Only James saw it, the paltry attempt to make her look as though the world had not touched her, beaten her up, and crushed the very life out of her. *Who did they think they were fooling?*

He glanced over at his parents. Ma was stoic, not a tear, unusual for her to be so tough, her rosary clenched in angry fists. Da was destroyed, bent down now on the kneeler in front of her casket, wringing out his very soul. Elsie, looking terrified for her parents and herself; the other boys, glum and solemn.

James thought about the dream he'd had last night during the few sleeping moments he'd had amongst the restlessness. He was high up in a burning building with no way down but to climb out a window and jump. Being too frightened, he waited. While waiting, several other people joined him in the room. Time was being devoured by the fire all around. Finally, in the midst of the conflagration, James spotted a doorway, invisible before this. He opened it and strode through to safety. It was only in the waiting that the answer came. *Is that all there is to it, then? Just the waiting?*

Father Cooney interrupted Jim's reverie with the intonation of the rosary. *Good,* thought James, *no one has to think now.* The family sank to their knees and followed the priest's drone.

At the turn of the twentieth century, journalists often wrote with great aplomb. The *Waterloo Daily Courier* was no exception:

> A thousand heavy hearted people attended the funeral of Miss Ella Condon, the victim of the streetcar accident at Sans Souci Park, at St. Joseph's Catholic Church yesterday afternoon at 2:30 o'clock;, and a very consoling discourse was preached by the pastor, Rev. Father Mark Cooney, one which acted as a balm to bleeding hearts.
>
> This was one of the largest funerals ever held in this church, and long before the time set for the services, a stream of people wended their way to the house of worship. When the cortege arrived from the Hanlon undertaking establishment with the body, the large and beautiful edifice was packed, but the people came in a stream. The gallery was packed, the entranceway to the auditorium was filled with folks that were standing and dozens stood at the back of the pews.
>
> The white casket in which all that was mortal of Miss Condon lay encased, was covered with a wealth of white blossoms, emblematic of the purity of life of the deceased.
>
> The members of the Woodmen of the World attended the services in a body out of respect to the father of the girl, who is a member of the order.
>
> Father Cooney spoke simply and tenderly of the life of the one who met such a tragic death, saying that she had partaken of her first holy communion about five years ago, following a course of instruction and training in things divine. He said she had been told of the significance of the rites of the church and had been taught the desirability of a Christian life. At that time, Miss Condon received her second birth – the birth that fits one for entrance into and occupancy of, the land of the redeemed, where her soul is now reveling in the bliss provided for all faithful sons and daughters of the church. He said she was told that life would be a battle, that the hosts of the evil one would assault her, that even Peter denied his Lord, but if she would only trust in Christ, who exemplified the union of the divine and the human, and would partake of the sacraments regularly, she could put to flight all of the enemies of her soul. The serene, peaceful, pure life of the girl speaks in eloquent phrase of how closely she kept to her Master.
>
> In addressing the members of the family so greatly bereaved, Father Cooney said he presumed his sympathy could best be expressed by that eloquent

silence where friend communes with friend, but he desired to call their attention to some of the passages of scripture which bring solace in such experiences as this. Then the pastor made a number of quotations and closed with a prayer.

The casket was opened and the large throng of sympathizing friends were given an opportunity to look upon the features of one who had for many years been a devout worshipper at St. Joseph's. A half hour was consumed in emptying the church, and it was noticed that the mist of emotion was visible on almost every eye, while most of the girls of the age of the deceased gave way to weeping. It was one of the saddest of funerals and one where sympathy and love were displayed in remarkable measure. While the streams of people were slowly treading their way down the broad center aisle with tear-dimmed eyes, the sweet voices of the schoolchildren from Our Lady of Victory Academy were lifted in song. Clear, sweet and melodious the tones of the hymns came forth like the liquid notes from the throats of larks. "Lead kindly Light, amid the encircling gloom" came the hopeful injunction as the children sang in stately chorus that old hymn which has often been the cause of rifting the cloud of darkness and letting the blessed sunshine come in.

After the cortege started for the cemetery, with the grief of the parents almost bursting their hearts, elderly folk and little children and representatives of all of the ages between, lingered in front of the church and looked their loneliness in the direction of the disappearing procession. Two aged ladies, bent with years, wept on each other's shoulder, and a little grandson tugged at their skirts and said in pained tones, "She didn't look so pretty as she used to, but I love her just the same." And then the aged mothers in Israel, waiting for the vesper hour, cuddled the boy and explained about the hurts the young lady had received.

East 4th St. between Franklin and Mulberry

CHAPTER 8

Wilbur Francis Condon

July 26, 1888-November 14, 1942

*"Dad, the nuns want us to bring our pennies for the pagan baby
drive at school. Can we have some?" "You can adopt all
the pagan babies you want, just don't bring any of them home!"*

– Wilbur responding to his daughter's pleas for pennies, Circa 1935

Will muttered to himself as he leaned under yet another dairy cow. Milking first thing in the morning and often late into the evening was the structure around which Will's life operated. It used to be such a mundane job, but it didn't matter anymore because Will had just one thing on his mind these days, and that was a tiny redhead named Mary Kane.

Farm kids grow up knowing a lot about basic sex and procreation but little about human relationships. That would come later on with experience. Still, now that he knew Mary Kathryn Kane, every animal's urges and their resolution spoke volumes to him. He could not keep his eyes off the bull and the cows during rutting. Watching them made him weak in the knees and so strong in other places that he often had to wait half an hour or more to walk back up to the house! *Is it a sin to think about rutting with Mary,* he thought. *Of course it is. The priests and nuns make us think that everything natural is a sin.* I don't believe it. It's too beautiful to be a sin. Will had met

Mary Kane, aged twelve, just months before at a church social in Fairbanks, Iowa, where she lived on a farm with her large family. This tiny ginger-haired girl was the eldest of ten children and a spitfire to boot. She didn't have much time for Will that day, as she was kept busy rounding up her siblings.

Will noted that Mary's mother was pretty sour looking. *Probably German,* he thought to himself. Mary's Da, on the other hand, had a twinkle in his eye. As evidenced by ten children, Will figured John Kane to be a down-to-the-earth sort. *I'll steer clear of the mother and say hello to the da one of these days,* thought Will. In the meantime, Will would ask his sister, Ellie, to mention his name to Mary Kane. *Girls were better at this,* he surmised. Ellie was fond of her younger brother and agreed to introduce him to Mary, though Will, with his sense of humor and good looks, was likely to win Mary over all by himself.

The century, in 1904, was still new; and life was quickly changing. Will had his heart set on working for the railroad like his brother Jack. Like James, he wanted to be off the farm for good. Da had done a good job providing for his family from the crops and cattle, but Will was no farmer. Leonard was the one who would go on farming. It suited him, as he was less of a people sort of person. Will could not see himself spending his days alone plowing fields or tending animals. He wanted to travel, to meet new people. Trains were the answer.

He knew that Mary was too young and would be in the care of her family for a few more years, but he was determined that she was the one for him and no one else would have her. Will could be a great charmer. He got that from Da. Da, the clown; Da, the dancer; Da, the singer; Da, the teaser; Da, everybody's friend. Will had been observing his father for years. He made it all seem easy, and Will was finding that it came natural to him as well. "Chipped off the old block," Ma called him.

Calvary Cemetery, Waterloo, Iowa

CHAPTER 9

The Inquest

The bustle in a house
The morning after death
Is solemnest of industries
Enacted upon earth

The sweeping up the heart,
And putting love away
We shall not want to use again
Until eternity.

– Emily Dickinson, 1830-1886

The parents and the remaining members of the family were almost prostrated by the news of Miss Ella's death. The young lady had been living in Waterloo only about a week which was the term of her employment at the home of Mr. Storm.

– *Waterloo Daily Courier,* Saturday evening, June 4, 1904

McManus knew that this next interview might very well reveal the vital piece in the puzzle of Miss` Condon's death. He was no detective, but he knew he must handle this delicately and with utmost finesse, or he might never discover the truth. Knowing almost nothing about the subject of his next interview put him at a distinct disadvantage. Not only had James not yet moved off the family farm, he would need to be interviewed on his own turf, because Mac had no idea if he ever left the farm or had any kind of social life at all. He would have to convince the young man that he needed his help. But how to get around the parents, that was the problem. He thought on it and decided to have his wife prepare baked goods, which he would deliver in person on the subterfuge of being in that part of the county on business of another kind. It had been only two days since the funeral, not a lot of time for this family to work through their grief, all the more reason to get fresh perspective.

The Condon farm was seven miles outside of Waterloo on the corner of Schenk and Dunkerton Roads. The highest point in the county, McManus had studied the plats in the recorder's office and knew just how much acreage Condon owned. He'd need that knowledge to locate James.

William Condon had purchased these 160 acres from John Stubbs on February 6, 1900, the northeast quarter of Section 32, Township 90, Range 12. Condon had prime acreage. *He was a busy farmer. With six sons and two daughters, everyone must have had a lot to do. Why would the eldest daughter leave to move into town? The younger girl was too young to pick up the chores Ella must have done. Little Elsie was only eight years old.*

Ella's place would have been with her mother, doing the cooking, cleaning, canning, chasing chickens away from the eggs, and feeding the potpourri of farm animals. Why did she leave? The question plagued McManus.

McManus headed over to the livery to collect his horse and buggy. The day was beginning to look grim. Storm clouds gathered in the west, threatening to send farmers in from their fields. *I need James alone, not surrounded by his family,* thought Mac as he neared the Dunkerton Road. Turning a wide right, Mac headed up the hill to the Condon farm. He noted that several men were out in the fields despite the threatening weather. Pray to God James was so engaged.

As he slowed his horse to enter the path leading into the farmyard, Mac spotted Mrs. Condon and her little daughter, Elsie, hanging wash on the line. Like an army of waving men, the shirtsleeves greeted and directed Mac up to the house.

Mary Condon started as she recognized the coroner. *She looks wretched,* thought McManus. Mary's eyes were nearly swollen shut, the color drained from her face so like Miss Ella's own, even in death. She began to weep as she approached the coroner. Pulling a well-used handkerchief from her apron, Mrs. Condon daubed at her eyes as she reached her guest.

McManus tethered his horse in front of the house and said, "Mrs. Condon, please forgive me for this unannounced call; but I was going to be in this part of the county today, and my wife insisted that I drop by to deliver these baked goods with her sympathy." "We're ever so grateful, Mr. McManus, how thoughtful of you and the missus. Please thank her for me."

Mac stood by awkwardly attempting to broach the topic of visiting with the men in the family, namely James. "If you could kindly point me in the direction where I might find your sons, I would like to take some of these goodies out to them." Mary looked at him quizzically but pointed to spots southwest and northeast of the house. "I'm afraid they are scattered about." Her voice trailed off, led into some dark place far from his presence. She turned and walked heavily back to her wash line, her retreating figure reminding him of someone well defeated by life.

As he turned to walk toward the barn and out to the fields, Mac spied a blonde head on the horizon. McManus knew it had to be James. All of the other family members had the black hair, even the deceased. He set off sprinting to the barn with a package of warm buns in one hand and a head full of questions, which threatened to overwhelm the receiver. *Calm down*, McManus told himself, *let's not frighten him into silence.*

James had stopped at the trough to kick the mud off his boots and did not see McManus until the latter was nearly on top of him. "Good day, James, is it?" queried Mac. Obviously startled, James rose up slowly to his full height and blushing full on red from head to toe, muttered, "It's Jim, thanks." McManus reached out and shook hands with the clearly flustered young man then handed Jim the package of warm rolls from his wife. "I'm sorry to bother you during your period of mourning, Jim, but I am needing to close the documentation on your sister's death; and I need to ask you some questions so as not to burden your parents. Would you be willing to help me out?" "You think I'm the one to do this?" answered Jim furtively. *Great*, thought Mac, *another question.*

He ignored it and replied, "Right then, is there a place we can talk where we'll not be interrupted?" Jim scanned the barnyard and then led McManus into the machine shed. Jim remained standing, but Mac pulled over a wooden stool and sat down. Jim had not yet made eye contact, and Mac was keenly aware of his hesitancy to do so.

Jim hadn't much appetite since Ella's death, but the warm buns smelled delicious. He was salivating, yet his stomach was roiling with nervous anticipation of what was coming next.

"James, er, Jim, you and Ella were just a year apart in age, is that correct?" "Yes," Jim mumbled so quietly that McManus barely heard his response. "Were you and your sister close, like confidantes?" The question hung in the humid summer air like a wet, dead stillness before a thunderstorm. All around the farm were the sounds of animals snorting, crowing, scratching, growing louder by the second as time hung still in the machine shed. James was in a terror. Hands clenched tightly into fists of brick and feeling trapped by the coroner, before he could stop himself, he blurted out angrily, "You can mind your own damned business. It's none of your affair! She's dead; she's not coming back."

Finally, Jim had raised his head to look directly into Mac's eyes. Mac was staring into an abyss of anger and grief. James flew from Mac's presence enraged and visibly shaken. *Well*, thought Mac, *I've obviously touched a nerve. Is it the results of the shock of Ella's death or something else or both?* Mac believed there was folly here that he needed to uncover, but it looked as though it was going to take lots of time and patience to unbury whatever ugly parasite was eating at this young man.

He decided to have a look around the farm to familiarize himself with Ella's home environment. The house itself was a cracker box, small, nothing special. *The family must be sleeping one atop the other,* thought Mac. The farm itself was a lone high spot with no neighbors for at least five miles. *Must be pretty bleak living for young people, but there are a lot of chores to keep them engaged.* Mac took out his notebook and pencil and began his tour.

CHAPTER 10

James, the Odd One

James was an enigma, even to himself. He never felt that he fit into the family. Ever the outsider peering in through the window of familial unity, James longed for something he could not name. He was nineteen now, old enough to be making plans for his future, but that future was hazy. While his brothers courted young women from the community, attending barn dances and church picnics, James remained isolated, withdrawn – what everyone else referred to as a "homebody."

While Irish men weren't known to rush into wedded bliss, James had little to no desire for such a thing. A girl had yet to catch his eye. Da kept hinting that he might want to look into some work in Waterloo, something that would peak his interest and move him on off the farm. Jim couldn't agree more about leaving the farm work. He hated it, but what else could he do? Where could he go?

Today, James was ready to explode. Full of grief, frustration, and anger at that McManus for intruding upon the sanctity of his family's pain. *How dare he. Who did he think he was?* And it wasn't just that, James wore guilt like his blushing countenance, ever visible to the world or anyone who might really care to look; but thank God, no one did, no one except, Ma, maybe. Sometimes, he felt her peering into his very soul. He and Ma were connected by their threads of sadness. She knew him, but she didn't know it all, not even he knew it all.

He hadn't slept well last night. He needed privacy, and there was none in the house. The boys all slept together in one room, two beds, three to a bed, foot to toe. No one was talking about the funeral, the accident, the loss, nothing. In his family, you picked up and kept moving, no time for brooding. *Time,* thought James, *a strange phenomenon. It's a human invention; either there's way too much of it or there's not nearly enough. People are always trying to "buy it," as though it were real.* For the Condons, planting and harvesting time – spring and fall, summer weeding time – all were full to overflowing with work. It was only in the Midwestern winter, when the days were stone-cold and short and the animals cared for, that time hung down heavy.

None felt this more than James. Time just exacerbated his problems. Restlessness ruled him. He lived with questions and terrors and did not seek the answers for fear of the outcomes. In one moment, he could be thoughtful and gentle; in the next, angry, cruel, and self-deprecating. He felt so bone sad most of the time. Ma called it "melancholia," the curse of the Irish. Da said it was nothing more than being a young man and learning to fill time well so it wouldn't overtake him.

His brothers called him "odd one out." Bernie tried to convince Jimmy that he'd been adopted, that Da had found him in a field and brought him home to Ma, that this was why his hair was blonde. Jimmy learned as he got older that Bernie was only pulling his leg, but it still hurt to feel the outsider. And he always felt the outsider.

James was drawn to his sisters – one, a year older; the other, eleven years younger. They made him feel more a part of things. They weren't so foreign and they were kind. Ma was good to him, too, but sometimes she looked at him with guilt as though his problems were somehow her fault. She made him uneasy in his own skin.

Unlike his younger brothers, James had no idea what he would do with his life beyond the fact that farming wasn't it. You couldn't make a living hunting and fishing and hiding out in the woods. If so, he'd be successful. He still had no girlfriend, not even a possibility, not even an urge. But lots of Irishmen are bachelors. He supposed he was headed that way, but not the kind that stays home and lives with his mother all of his life, not him, not ever.

CHAPTER II

The Inquest

*The Condon family are among the most prominent and
most highly respected in the county and the grief stricken relatives
have the sympathy of a wide circle of friends.*

– Waterloo Daily Courier, Saturday evening, June 4, 1904

McManus watched as James strode angrily back to the fields. Mary Condon was still busy hanging the wash, and from the looks of the pile, it would be a good while before she ventured into the house. *Just like the Irish,* he thought, *when tragedy strikes, you get busy.* Mac calmly let himself in the backdoor into a tiny back porch area full of muddy boots, hanging overalls, an aged rusty rifle, and all sundry accoutrements of farm living. The aroma of pig emanated from the boots at his feet, and Mac sought out his handkerchief to muffle the smell.

Stepping to his right, he entered a wee kitchen piled high with foodstuffs, most likely funeral alms from thoughtful neighbors. Now he could savor the aroma of steeped tea, warm bread, and last winter's sacrificial corncobs to the old cooking stove. A solid wooden table, two long benches, and two ladder-back chairs made up the furnishings. *Well crafted,* thought Mac, *not a nail in sight, all hand pegged. Someone's a good woodworker.* The stove with its stern pipe hat stood starkly against the rococo wallpaper, a silent sentinel to the life of this family. *That wallpaper is expensive,* he mused, *the only luxury item anywhere in sight, must be that William is a man to keep his wife happy.*

Small houses hold large secrets, thought Mac, as he poked around. *What was life like for Ella here with six brothers?* He'd heard stories in his years as coroner, stories no one wants to hear or acknowledge, unthinkable things. *Was this one of those? The thing people don't understand,* mused Mac, *is that darkness dissipates, and the light will get through. Things will be revealed, sometimes over lifetimes, but revealed they will be.*

Stepping to his left and entering the parlor, Mac moved furtively over to the window and peeked out at Mary Condon still mindlessly hanging wash. Never let it be said that the Irish don't use industry to further bury what they want hidden. Mary's face revealed a woman in an agony of grief, with little to no sleep to buoy her up, out doing her chores as though the world depended upon those clothes to be dried at once. The little girl, Elsie, sat near her mother, playing with a rag doll, tossing it up and down, twirling it to an unheard tune, dancing in barefooted innocence. *The extremes of womanhood,* thought Mac. No bent shoulders on Elsie, no permanent lines between her eyes or bulges under them, no heavy burdens breaking her back and heart.

The only sound in the house was the eerie ticking of a clock in the parlor. Mac was startled by a mouse running over his boot and into small a hole in the wall between the kitchen and parlor. He stepped into the main room of the house.

The parlor, or what was once that, now appeared to be a shrine to a young girl named Ellie. Besides a small horsehair-covered settee and two wooden chairs, the only other piece of furniture was a breakfront covered in memorabilia, wilting flowers, a photograph of a young dark-haired girl with a faraway look in her huge eyes. She appeared to be between twelve and sixteen years of age in the photo, he couldn't say for sure. She had the same wide full lips of her brothers. Her eyes were sad, as though she knew her fate well ahead of the event.

Studying the picture flashed Mac back to the Sans Souci Hotel where they brought Ella's body to be examined by Dr. Gollmar. She was so badly mutilated. He remembered how surprised he was to discover that the family had chosen to have an open casket at her funeral. After all, what a ghastly sight she'd been that night, with half her body twisted this way and the other that way – entrails exposed. Her friend, Miss Winninger, could only identify her by her clothing, certainly not by her features. But here in this parlor, in this shrine, she was pretty again – whole and unsullied by the wheels of interurban no. 23.

Her visage haunted Mac. He felt that she was trying to tell him something, something vital to his investigation, but what was it? The dead don't speak, but those they leave behind do and will, by god. Suddenly, Mac was startled by the banging of the backdoor. He quickly returned the picture to its place of prominence and spun around to meet his detector. His eyes fell three feet to encounter a tiny girl of eight years looking up at him. She said nothing but was holding something behind her back.

"Mammy sent me in for clothes pegs," she blurted out defensively. "Please don't tell her about the bun." Elsie was shielding a bun in her small hand as she glanced up at Mac. "We'll make it our secret," he replied to his co-conspirator. "What is your name, miss?" "I'm Elsie, who are you?" "I'm Mr. McManus, and I need your help. Would you be after showing me where you sleep, young Elsie?" Elsie dashed ahead up a narrow staircase between the kitchen and the parlor. Mac followed. At the top of the steps to the right were three rooms. Elsie ran to the last and threw open the door to what appeared to be her parents' room. "I used to sleep with Ellie, but she's gone now, and I sleep in Mammy and Da's room." A small pallet on the floor confirmed her story.

Mac bent down to enter the room. The parents' room was the smallest and least furnished in the house. A pole extended from one corner to the opposite to hold the folk's meager collection of clothes. Mac spied a familiar bundle sticking out from under the bed, a bundle wrapped with newspaper and tied with twine, the very bundle in which he'd wrapped their daughter's bloody clothing. *There's one load of wash she's missed*, thought Mac darkly. It seemed macabre to him that Mary would keep this in such an intimate space. A small chiffonier sat in the corner by the window.

Mac turned quickly to Elsie and said, "Show me the room you used to sleep in." Elsie moved to the second room and opened the door to what can only be described as second shrine. A cast – iron bed covered with straw ticking; and a quilt was laid out with two dresses, a hat, two pairs of shoes, a pair of gloves, a purse, three handkerchiefs, a nightgown – all the makings of what might once have been a lovely trousseau. Along the wall was a wooden closet with three small drawers. He thanked Elsie then reminded her to take the pegs to her mother. "I won't tell about the bun if you don't tell that I am in the house, okay?" "Okay," she replied as she backed down the steps.

Mac quickly opened the closet and the drawers. Finding only little girls' things, he desperately searched for a diary, a letter, anything that might reveal clues to this mystery. *Nothing*, thought Mac, *absolutely nothing, but what did I expect? If there was something revealing, it would have been long removed by now. Does the mother know something*, he pondered. *If so, she hides it well behind her grief.* McManus knew enough about the Irish to know that if there was anything shameful here, Mary would be the last to reveal it and the first to bury it. An Irish woman never reveals her family's business.

He returned to the parents' room and began to rifle through the chiffonier. He found ladies' gloves, undergarments, holy cards and rosaries, but nothing revealing or incriminating.

Mac closed the door and climbed furtively down the steps and back into the kitchen to find Mary Condon waiting for him. "Please, sir, what would you be looking for inside my house?" Mac spotted Elsie behind her mother's skirt and thought, *The little snitch. Well, maybe she's the healthiest one in this house, no dirty little secrets there.*

"Mrs. Condon," he began, "I was concerned that there might be more clues to learn about Miss Ella's accident." "Clues, what do you mean, clues? Are you telling me this might not have been an accident?" Mary's voice rose hysterically as she spoke, and she dissolved into wailing right before Mac's eyes. "No no, Mrs. Condon, I'm not saying that. I just want to be sure that we have checked all the possibilities, because the inquest was inconclusive. That is all. I am so sorry to have disturbed you in your time of grief. Please forgive me. I'll be taking my leave now. Please give my best to your husband."

McManus exited the house, climbed into his hansom, and left the farm before any more Condons could confront him. *Gads,* he thought, *there is a tyranny of self-protection in this family.*

CHAPTER 12

Elsie, 1896-1925

One potato, two potatoes, three potatoes four.

– Children's jump-roping rhyme

*I*t's all Mammy's fault, thought Elsie, as she followed her mother back from the house and out to the clothesline. *Ellie would still be here if Mammy hadn't let her go off to Waterloo. Mammy kept saying that the house was too small, and the big kids needed to move out to give us all some stretching room, but she didn't mean Ellie. She meant the boys. Well, maybe, she meant the boys, maybe not. Mammy's partial to her boys.*

Little Elsie was just beginning to feel her loss. A big sister is an important person in the life of a small girl. Just peeking into their shared bedroom made Elsie's chest feel heavy and her tummy sick. She missed her big sister. She began to think about her last days with Ellie as she helped Ma hang the wash.

Ellie was so quiet like, strange, not very friendly that last week at home. She stared a lot at something out there and barely heard me when I spoke to her. She was jumpy, restless, not her happy self. Elsie remembered thinking that maybe Ellie was tired of them all and wanted to get away. Elsie's only other playmate was Jim. He listened to her like Ellie used to do. *He's more like a sister than a brother,* thought Elsie, *playing house with me, chasing the kitties in the barn until he catches one and hands it over to me ever so gently with his great, big hands. He's different from the other boys who are all rough and tumble. Will tickles me 'til I cry, and Mammy has to yell at him to leave me be. Bernie wrestles me to the ground. Carl calls me "stinky" and hides my dolls all over the barn. Jack and Leonard are like Da. They give me rides up on their shoulders and let me steer the tractor when they're plowing or planting.*

Elsie knew that she was pampered by the men in her life. Being the youngest had its advantages. Da loved to play games with her, and she loved to make him laugh, especially when he came in from the fields tired and hungry. Da never picked her up until he washed. Not like the brothers who'd smother her with hugs just after leaving the pigpen. Whew! The stink was awful, and it made Elsie so angry that they rubbed it off on her. That's one thing her brothers gave her, an awful temper! They encouraged her outbursts with their merciless teasing. They never treated Ellie like that because she was older and she fought back.

But Ellie was dead. Young Elsie knew death. She'd seen it countless times on the farm, lifeless creatures with blank eyes staring up at nothing. Ellie's eyes were closed to make it look like she was sleeping. But she hadn't moved when Elsie snuck her hand into the casket and shook her arm, so Elsie knew her sister was dead.

"Mammy, will I get dead?" Elsie suddenly spoke aloud the thoughts that were consuming her. Ma stopped short and with shoulders slumped under her invisible burden, stooped down to take Elsie into her embrace. "Oh, child, we all die. None of us gets out of this world and into the next alive." "When will I die?" asked Elsie with a trembling lower lip. "Not for a long, long time, not until you're an old, old lady," replied Ma. "But Ellie wasn't old!" shouted Elsie as she turned and ran away from her mother's crushing arms.

CHAPTER 13

Ma, 1859-1938

Mary, Mary, quite contrary, how does your garden grow?
With silver bells and cockle shells and pretty maids all in a row.

– Children's nursery rhyme

Mary Meagher Curran hadn't had an easy life, not by a long shot; but this time was the worst of it all, having to bury a grown child. Her parents had been struggling Irish immigrants who made it out of Ireland just after the first of several famines which plagued that beautiful land. How Mary's mother had mourned her family back home in Queen's County, so much so that she'd little time for her own children, who pretty much raised themselves. Mary's Da, Michael Curran, was a farmer much like William, with a sense of humor. She still missed him dearly. Ellen Meagher, Mary's mother, had died in 1893; and Michael Curran, her father, in 1898, after long lives spent creating a new world for themselves in America.

Mary often wondered why her parents were so reluctant to speak of the famine in Ireland. She knew they grieved it; but like most immigrants of the time, they put on a stoic face and went forward, leaving it all behind. *But where does it go once left behind?* thought Mary. Like love, does it grieve on from generation to generation? Why did the grim God not take her love for Ellie along with Ellie so this darkness would dissipate? Had her mother not felt this, her father? The love that stays alive and well and eats away at one's insides for sustenance, a parasite destroying the very host that birthed it.

Mary could see this in her own children, the darkness, she called it the "melancholia." She feared that James was intimate with it. Her parents always told her to keep on smiling and everything would be okay. It didn't work, but it made her parents feel better. They needn't pay so much attention to her darkness if she smiled.

Ma had given birth to her first child at age twenty-five and her last at thirty-seven, all in all, eleven pregnancies. Every one brought her down a bit further into the chasm. After birthing her last boy in 1894, Mary called a halt to William's privileges. She was exhausted and nearly unable to lift herself from the bed to tend to the family. William was not to have the pleasure of her honor again for sometime. She'd felt guilty, her mother's words ringing in her ears to be a "good Catholic wife and never refuse your husband his rights." She could not bear it. Her next child would not appear until 1896, and she wrestled with her guilt daily about that.

When Mary confessed to the priest, as she did weekly, this was the sin she tried to slip in quietly among the others, hoping that he'd miss its significance. But he always remanded her to be "a good, dutiful wife" and to "welcome the children God sends you." Mary was too destroyed from lack of sleep, a deep-down restlessness, and the chores of daily life on the farm. William just had to wait. And now, he'd wait again and more, perhaps forevermore.

CHAPTER 14

Da, 1851-1916

To be Irish is to know that the world will break your heart
before you're forty.

– Author unknown

William Condon had been out in the fields all morning, weeding. The boys were helping, but it was a long, tedious job. Some days he wished he'd had more sons so the jobs could be completed sooner. His eight, now seven, children were the joy and sorrow of his life. There were more, but three had died in infancy; and these days there was little hope for more as Mary had cut him off a long time ago, and they were getting old. Elsie was the result of a weak moment or a sympathy gesture on Mary's part. She'd married him when she was twenty-five. She was a real beauty back then, with her thick black hair and big blue eyes.

He missed the intimacy and the purely animal pleasure of entering his wife. He sometimes envied his animals who took what they needed when they needed it. *How pathetic a man I am*, thought William, *to be thinking such things just after burying my child.* Trying to lose himself in the work of the day put off the inevitable grieving left to be done, but he was good at distracting himself.

William was funny. A natural wit, he was a great foil for his wife's solemnity. He played tricks on his children and delighted in their reactions. Like the time Jack got a lump of coal in his Christmas stocking for daring to suggest that there was no Father Christmas. Or Allhallows Eve, when William dressed up as a hobo and went all over the county to the doors of his neighbors begging for food. No one recognized him, and every one fed him! He loved Halloween, his favorite holiday with its roots all the way back to Ireland. For all of their melancholia, the Irish had so much of the faerie spirit that they overflowed with mischief and a sense of fun. Sometimes you had to dig deep to find it, but it was always worth the time and trouble.

William Condon had a soft spot for his animals, so much so that he named them nearly one and all. The only ones who remained unnamed were the chickens, and only because they were too numerous – and too often supper – to be attached to a name. His affinity for all living things translated to the plant life as well. William never felled a tree without planting two in its place.

"C'mere, Bozee," he called out, and sure enough, a ram ran right up to the fence to greet him. "Nanny" followed with her twins, and all got a good nuzzle from William. "Here you go, have a treat," he called out to the lambs as he pulled a long-nippled bottle of milk from his overalls pocket. The lambs took turns tugging on the nipple through the fence, nearly pulling William's arm out of its socket. Once they got the last bit of sweet warm milk, the fickle lambs leapt off after their mother and left William sitting in the remnants of sweet clover. Sweet clover always gave William a lazy, heady feeling. He gathered a handful of the tiny flowers to bring back to Mary's dinner table, but he couldn't seem to get up off the ground.

Ellie was there all around him. He'd always called her "Mrs. McGillacuddy." "Mrs. McGillacuddy, would you be after fetching me a cup of water from the pump?" he'd ask. Her nickname came to him when she was just an infant. She'd always looked so serious, even as a babe, studying everyone with her big eyes and frowning mightily like a little old "Mrs. McGillicuddy."

His mind wandered back to last Christmas Eve. Ma had made oyster stew from the oysters he and Ellie had purchased at Booth's Meat Market in Waterloo. She loved it, though he'd reminded her that her first taste, back when she was little, made her gag mightily. He smiled at the memory.

It was warm sitting here in the clover. He wasn't ready to leave this little Eden for the stuffiness of the house and all of its dark memories. He rose and wandered over to the chicken house to secure it for the night. He coaxed the chickens inside then closed up the doors to protect the hens from roaming foxes and coyotes, the worst chickennappers in the county. He was bone tired tonight and would not welcome the rising din should the raiding prowlers appear.

William was not looking forward to going into the house for supper. Mary was a caution. He didn't know how to comfort her, and even if he did, she would not accept the attention. She just kept working, tiring herself out. He knew that didn't help her get to sleep at night. They both tossed and turned last night, all night long. He'd tried saying the rosary in bed, gripping the beads, and passing them one by one through his calloused hands, fingering the rote prayers. Even the repetition gave him no comfort, no rest. His wife's body, so warm and restive beside him, caused not a tingle of energy in him. His Ellie was gone, and no amount of comfort would return her to her da.

Taking one last long look around the farmyard, William collected the sweet clover bouquet and headed for the house.

CHAPTER 15

The Inquest

Melancholia: mental disease characterized
by great depression of spirits and gloomy forebodings.

– The Random House Dictionary of the English Language

B ack in his office, Mac cleared the desk and spread his notes out in front of him. He poured himself a whiskey from a bottle in the bottom drawer of his desk, clearly frustrated by the unsatisfactory encounters at the Condon farm. There were no messages left under the door. *Good*, thought Mac, *I need to think*.

Sipping on his whiskey, Mac had more questions than answers still. *What are the Condons hiding? Are they hiding anything? Or do they have as many questions as I?* While it is not unusual for Irish families to create shrines to their dead, why were there no letters, diaries, musings, nothing left in Ella's own hand? Someone in that family knows something, he was sure of it.

Mac stared at the sash of the door pondering No Messages Left.

Pulling out a sheet of paper and a pencil, Mac made several columns and began to write down what he knew:

1. Miss Ella leaves the farm at age eighteen to go to work as a domestic in the city.
2. Mary Condon needs the help of an older daughter on the farm.

3. James becomes defensive and refuses to talk about his relationship with Miss Ellie.
4. Ellie appears to have become depressed and distant in the days leading to her departure for Waterloo.
5. There are no visible clues left at the farm to explain her departure.
6. There is yet no eyewitness account to her death.
7. There are no notes left in her hand.

I wonder, thought Mac, *is it possible that the young lady might have found suicide more palatable in the anonymous than in the familiar?* McManus thought seriously that Miss Ella may have been far more clever than he was giving her credit for, especially considering that not one of the horde at the band concert could positively say they saw what happened. Miss Ella must have had some power in the family as well because she talked them into letting her go.

Was she suffering from melancholia? In Mac's experience, melancholia occurred when people stuffed feelings like fear, anger, guilt, regret, or hatred. When they could no longer deal with them, they tended to go into this state of melancholy, a shocklike state where the feelings hide.

Well, this would take this case down another avenue all together. A suicide would certainly cause more questions than answers. It would put the family on the defensive, as their religion strictly forbids suicide to the point of condemning a person to hell for all eternity. Mac thought he might be onto something, but he also understood that this was not to be proven. Miss Ella may have been a very clever young woman indeed.

What might have caused her so much pain? Was she feeling hopeless? Was there a young man somewhere who spurned her? Ellie, thought Mac, *I wish you could speak to me. Were you protecting someone?* Mac wished more than ever that they had done an autopsy. It would have concluded Miss Ella's purity or otherwise.

Are some things best left buried? Nothing he could do would bring her back anyway. If there were someone out there who was directly responsible for pushing Miss Ella onto the tracks, surely he would be found out sooner or later, either through words misspoken or guilty conscience. Mac found it hard to believe that anyone could go to his or her death without revealing something this profound, unless, of course, it drove them crazy and they ended up in the loony bin.

Mac tended toward his suicide theory now more than anything else, including the possibility that it may have been an "accident." The accident theory did not add up for him. He wished so much that he had met Miss Ella. He may have been able to discern whether this was a very bright, calculating young woman or a very despondent, desperate one. Either way, Mac believed more and more that she probably staged her own demise to look like an accident and thereby save her family face.

He finished his whiskey, closed his notebook, and strode out the door for home, feeling a bit lighter and less responsible to reach a more definitive answer. Life would go on, time would heal and Miss Ella's memory would fade. Why, in a few years, no one would even know she'd ever lived at all.

James Condon's gravestone

CHAPTER 16

Eleven Years Later: James

Though leaves are many, the root is one;
Through all the lying days of my youth
I swayed my leaves and flowers to the sun;
Now I may wither into the truth.

– W. B. Yeats, 1865-1939

Mae McCarville, my cousin, told me that the Condons reported to the coroner
and the newspaper that James was killed accidentally while out hunting,
because they wanted him to be buried in the Catholic cemetery. You know, they
didn't bury suicides in holy ground back then.

– Dorothy Condon Paar, eldest daughter of Wilbur Condon

James Michael Condon – 30 years, 4 months, 7 days
Birthplace: DeKalb County, Illinois – March 7, 1885
Death: 7 miles outside of Waterloo, Iowa, July 14, 1915
DEATH CAUSED BY GUNSHOT WOUND
WEAPON ACCIDENTALLY DISCHARGED, KILLING JAS. CONDON
Second tragic Death Recorded in Family of William Condon

– *Waterloo Daily Courier,* July 15, 1915

M odern science has proven that lightning can certainly strike in the same place more than once. Unfortunately, the Condons were about to learn this tragic lesson.

> James M. Condon, a well-known young farmer of Bennington Township, was instantly killed yesterday when the shotgun, which he was carrying, was accidentally discharged. He had left the house about 1 p.m. and had walked about a half mile from home. While attempting to crawl through a barbed-wire fence, the gun was in some way discharged. The charge entered the body near the heart, and the young man's death was instantaneous. The tragedy occurred on the Stubbs farm about six miles northwest of the city.
>
> The death occurred early in the afternoon, it is believed, the body was not discovered until about 6:30 p.m. The young man's younger sister, Elsie, made the discovery. She had gone to town about three o'clock in the afternoon and had seen him lying there by the fence. She even saw the stains of blood on the clothing but thought it was paint and that the man was sleeping. When she returned from town and found him still lying there in the same position, she went to investigate. The shock of finding her brother dead nearly prostrated her.
>
> Mr. Condon was thirty years of age and the son of Mr. and Mrs. William Condon, highly respected residents of Bennington. This is the second tragic death in their family. A daughter, Helen [Ella] was killed about nine [eleven] years ago at Sans Souci Park when a car backed into a crowd of people who were trying to board the interurban car.
>
> The parents of the young man were in a state of collapse today following their son's death. The deceased was much beloved by all who knew him because of his sunny disposition and cheerful manner, and the news of his death was a shock to everyone in that locality.
>
> Mr. Condon was born in DeKalb County, Illinois on March 7, 1885, and came to Black Hawk in 1890. He is survived by his parents, five brothers, and one sister. The brothers are John L., Wilbur F., Bernard P., Leonard, and Carl, all of whom – also the sister, Elsie – live in this locality.
>
> The coroner was called to view the remains, but he pronounced the death accidental and no inquest was held. The body was removed to the O'Keefe and Towne Undertaking Parlors to be prepared for burial.
>
> Funeral services will be held in St. Joseph's Church Friday morning at 9:30. The funeral party will leave the home for the church at 8:30. Interment will take place in Calvary Cemetery.

It would be at least sixty years after this event that a conversation took place between Mae McCarville and Dorothy Condon Paar – Wilbur's cousin and daughter, respectfully. The former related the true story to her cousin Dorothy. It seems that the Condon family – in order to bury James in the Catholic cemetery, at that time considered "holy ground" – invented the story of a "hunting accident," rather than deal with the shame of a suicide in the family.

Poor James, not only unknown during his lifetime but denied his final decision and its action by the family who sought to protect him and themselves from scandal – a fragmented life and death lost, until now.

James Michael Condon's death certificate from book 3, page 352, no. 7804, in the death records of Black Hawk County Recorder's Office:

> James Michael Condon – 30 yrs., 4 mos., 7 days
> Birthplace: (DeKalb County) Illinois, March 7, 1885
> Death: Bennington Township July 14, 1915
> "Accidental discharge of a shotgun through his heart"
> Sidney D. Smith, Coroner
> Undertaker: O'Keefe & Towne
> Burial: Calvary Cemetery, July 16, 1915

Elsie was nineteen years old and, unlike her older sister, still living at home. Odd that she should see her brother's bloody body lying on the ground and make no attempt to discover the circumstances until returning from town hours later. Or was this part of the cover-up? The Condons were great storytellers, even in their grief, especially in their grief. Perhaps Elsie's story had given them time to create the circumstances of Jim's death so as to throw off any suspicion of suicide.

The news account refers to Jim's "sunny disposition and cheerful manner." Was this part of the family's concoction or was Jim, like many despairing people, able to put on a false face to the world around him?

Melancholia, despair, depression, despondency all have a genetic root. Unresolved, un-medicated, unacknowledged, they may pass onto the coming generations. Speaking the truth, naming the demon, and acknowledging this as all part of the human condition can break the cycle. As Ella so eloquently mused, perhaps we were never meant to be perfect, for if we were, we would not need one another.

Ella and Jim's legacy to the following generations of their family and to anyone who takes the time to read this book is that very lesson: Speak your truth, feel your feelings, seek help, be yourself, make better choices.

CHAPTER 17

Six Months Later:
William "Da" Condon

Death Certificate, book 3, page 374, number 7443
Black Hawk County Recorder's Office
William Condon
Born: Milwaukee, Wisconsin, January 12, 1851
Died: Bennington Township, January 31, 1916
Cerebral Hemorrhage; Arteriosclerosis
Buried: Calvary Cemetery, February 2, 1916

– Waterloo Evening Courier and Reporter, Tuesday, Feb. 1, 1916

WILLIAM CONDON DIES OF PARALYSIS

WELL KNOWN BENNINGTON TOWNSHIP FARMER IS DEAD
Survived by Widow and His Children

William Condon, age about 65 years and well-known farmer of Black Hawk County, died at his home in Bennington Township, eight miles northeast of Waterloo at 3 o'clock yesterday afternoon. Death was caused by paralysis by which he was first stricken about a year ago. [Perhaps following the suicide of his son?] Two subsequent strokes followed, the last occurring Sunday, which left him in a critical condition. It was realized after the last attack that he could not survive long.

Deceased was a successful farmer and generally beloved by his neighbors and all who knew him. He had been a resident of Black Hawk County for the past 24 years.

He was born in Milwaukee and, while still an infant, moved with his parents, to a farm near DeKalb, Illinois, where he grew to manhood. His marriage to Miss Mary Curran took place in Waterloo in 1884. The widow survives together with the following children: John, Carl and Elsie, all at home. Bernard P., Leonard and Wilbur, all of whom, reside in Waterloo. One sister, Mrs. John Moore, resides at DeKalb, Illinois and two nieces, Mrs. T. E. Kelly and Mrs. M. J. Horan, reside here.

Funeral Plans

> Funeral services will be held at 9:30 o'clock Wednesday morning from St.
> Joseph's Catholic Church and interment will be made in the family plot in
> Calvary Cemetery.

There are those who believe that if one does not listen to one's spirit, the body will make him or her listen. A body never loses the struggle between spirit and itself. As if losing his children, Ella and James, to great tragedy wasn't enough, William's body began to manifest those paralyzing losses through his own physical manifestation and by way of paralyzing strokes no less.

The obituary alludes to the fact that first of these strokes hit William "about a year ago." James's suicide occurred on July 15, 1915. Was William ill at the time or did he suffer from the stroke following James's death? We do not know, but we do know that his soul's experience of the deaths of his children impacted his body's ability to carry any more loss.

Elsie's Home at 216 Mullan Avenue

CHAPTER 18

Nine Years Later: Elsie

Elsie F. Condon Kelley
Born: June 16, 1896
Died: In childbirth, August 25, 1925

– Waterloo Courier, August 26, 1925

Mrs. T. S. Kelley, 29, of 216 Mullan Ave. East, died at 3:00 a.m. at St. Francis Hospital, Waterloo of Eclampsia. She is survived by her infant daughter, Jean Marie. Born June 16, 1896, she lived all of her life in the county. She was educated at Our Lady of Victory Academy and was a lifetime member of St. Joseph's Catholic Church. She was always a favorite among school and church associates because of her sunny and cheerful disposition.

Her marriage to Mr. Kelley occurred June 14, 1924. Surviving besides husband and infant child are her mother, Mrs. Mary Condon residing at the family home and these brothers: J. L., W. F., B. P. Condon, all of Waterloo; Leonard, East Waterloo Township, and C. M., Bennington Township.

Elsie Condon's infant daughter, Jean Marie, died at the age of six weeks.

Lamb at grave

On what was purported to be one of the happiest days of her life, Elsie, while delivering her infant, died of eclampsia or toxemia, characterized by convulsions, at the age of twenty-nine. Was Elsie composed of delicate design or was this yet another chapter in the long sad saga of the Condon family?

How did their mother, Mary Condon, handle this – both the death of her youngest child and last daughter and the death of her little granddaughter? Family history indicates that she kept house for Tom Kelley, Elsie's husband, for several years. Perhaps she had the care of her tiny granddaughter for those six weeks following Elsie's death as well.

Mary Condon left Tom's house when he remarried (Harriet Wendling) and eventually lived with Wilbur and Mary Kane Condon and their seven children.

CHAPTER 19

Thirteen Years Later:
Mary "Ma" Condon

Mary Curran Condon
Born: January 23, 1859 – Rockford, Illinois
Died: August 19, 1938 – Waterloo, Iowa

– Waterloo Sunday Courier, August 21, 1938

When you are old and grey and full of sleep,
And nodding by the fire, take down this book,
And slowly read, and dream of the soft look
Your eyes had once, and of their shadows deep;

How many loved your moments of glad grace,
And loved your beauty with love false or true
But one man loved the pilgrim soul in you,
And loved the sorrows of your changing face;

And bending down beside the glowing bars,
Murmur, a little sadly, how Love fled
And paced upon the mountain overhead
And hid his face amid a crowd of stars.

– William Butler Yeats, 1864-1939

S ervices for Mrs. Mary A. Condon who lived in Bennington Township, Black Hawk County, for nearly sixty eight [48] years, will be at 9:00 a.m. Monday from St. Joseph's Catholic Church. She died at 9:30 p.m. Friday at the home of a son, W. F. Condon, 415 Iowa Street, after a three-month illness of complication due to advanced age. She was 79 years old.

Mary Condon, daughter of Michael and Ellen Curran, was born on January 23, 1859, in Rockford, Illinois. In 1870, she accompanied her parents to this county. On April 21, 1884, she was married to William Condon. Her husband and three children – James M., Ellie M. [A.], and Mrs. Elsie Condon Kelley – preceded her in death.

Surviving are five sons, 23 grandchildren, and one sister, Mrs. Elizabeth Barron, 217 First Street East. The sons are John L., 124 Parker Street; Carl, Jesup, Iowa; Leonard, on the old home farm; Wilbur F., 415 Iowa Street; and Bernard, El Paso, Texas.

The body was taken to the O'Keefe and Towne Funeral Home. It will be returned to the residence at 415 Iowa Street this afternoon. The family requests that no flowers be sent.

Casket bearers will be: Herman Daugherty, Henry McGlaughlin, Frank Smith, Joseph Ryan, James Sims, and Thomas Daugherty.

The irony of having lived into old age, Mary Condon had shouldered more loss – the worst kinds of loss – in those earlier years. Yet despite those losses and her own innate sadness, she must have found life worth living and others in her life worth living for well into her eightieth year. She could have written the book on loss, grief, and survival. Instead, she lived it, and that is her legacy.

My grandmother, Mary Kane Condon, cared for Mary in her old age. When asked by her youngest daughter why she did this, considering that there were Wilbur, Mary, and seven children in a small two-bedroom house, Mamie replied, "Because no one else would take her. She was very unkind to me."

AFTERWORD

Long years apart can make no breach a second cannot fill
The absence of the witch does not invalidate the spell.
The embers of a thousand years uncovered by the hand
That fondled them when they were fire
Will stir and understand.

— Emily Dickinson, 1830-1886

For at least the past twenty-five years, there has been a song plaguing my days and nights, like the tune that sticks in your mind long after the initial exposure. After discovering Ella's story, I often wondered if it might have been the last song she ever heard. Perhaps it was the closing song of the band concert that evening at Sans Souci. I did some research and found that "After the Ball" was written in Milwaukee, Wisconsin, in 1892 by Charles K. Harris. It could easily have been on the bill of fare that summer evening in 1904. Did this audio haunting have a message for me?

The lyrics appear below with the standout lines in boldface, the lines that set me reeling with questions and intrigue.

A little maiden climbed an old man's knee –
Begged for a story, "Do Uncle, please!
Why are you single, why live alone?
Have you no babies, have you no home?"

"I had a sweetheart, years, years ago,
Where she is now, pet, you will soon know;
List to the story, I'll tell it all:
I believed her faithless, after the ball."

After the ball is over, after the break of morn,
After the dancers' leaving, after the stars are gone,
Many a heart is aching, if you could read them all –
Many the hopes that have vanished after the ball.

"Bright lights were flashing in the grand ballroom,
Softly the music, playing sweet tunes.
There came my sweetheart, my love, my own,
'I wish some water; leave me alone.'

When I returned, dear, there stood a man,
Kissing my sweetheart as lovers can.
Down fell the glass, pet, broken that's all –
Just as my heart was after the ball."

After the ball is over, after the break of morn,
After the dancers leaving, after the stars are gone,
Many a heart is aching, if you could read them all –
Many the hopes that have vanished, after the ball.

"Long years have passed, child, I have never wed,
True to my lost love though she is dead.
She tried to tell me, tried to explain –
I would not listen, pleadings were vain.

One day a letter came from that man;
He was her brother, the letter ran.
That's why I'm lonely, no home at all –
I broke her heart, pet, after the ball. (emphasis mine)

The song left me with a passel of unanswered questions:

Am I the only one who would find it odd that a brother would be kissing his sister "as lovers can?" Was she trying to reveal something of her dilemma to me? If there was an incestuous relationship, then which brother were we talking about? Was the "odd one" just too odd for this? Why did she leave the house, to escape him? Was she already in too deep? Was she pregnant? Did the family pump up her "goodness" to ensure that she would be buried in "holy ground?" Did the family even know? If so, what did they know? What did she choose to tell them? On the night of the concert, in the marauding crowd, was there a certain someone who pushed her to avoid having the truth revealed? Or to save herself and her family the shame, did Miss Ella purposefully walk onto that train track? Why did her brother, James, commit suicide eleven years later?

I have had a fascination with trolleys since I was a tiny girl. I remember riding on one with my grandmother, Mary Kane Condon, Will's wife. I have such a vivid memory of that, but my own mother tells me that the trolleys were gone by the time I was born in 1949.

I remember back in the 1980's calling my eldest aunt, Dorothy, Wilbur's oldest child, who knew of Ella's death but, of course, had never known her. I took a big risk talking to my auntie about the "haunting." After all, she might think this niece had gone 'round the bend. She listened respectfully then replied, "Judy, thank God you felt her trying to reach you. She's probably been trying to reach through one of us for years to tell her story."

That is when I began to research her life and death. I went to the old Sans Souci Park and talked with her in my heart, begging her to use me to emote so that her spirit could rest. I went to the church where she'd been buried and I'd been married. I sat at her grave in Calvary Cemetery. I found her farm home, seven miles outside of Waterloo, and introduced myself to the present owners, who were gracious enough to let me poke around their property.

I paid close attention to the number of "Ellas" I met over those years when I had set aside thinking about the haunting. She did not let up.

I spent hours at the Black Hawk County Recorder's Office, the Grout Museum Genealogical Library, and the Waterloo Public Library poring over documents. I figured that I would know when I'd done enough, because her spirit would surely let up on me. I found it intriguing and eerily appropriate that the only two years of missing documentation between 1880 and 2006 in the Black Hawk County Recorder's Office were 1903 and 1904. No one in the office had any idea why those years were missing.

I prowled through antique stores in the city seeking clues. I hovered over handmade quilts and crocheted doilies wishing they might speak to me and reveal who had been born, who had died, who had loved and cried and grieved under the former, and who had woven love and tears into the latter.

Sometimes I wonder if they are all back here now living around me, interacting every day, having chosen new lives, wishing to resolve the old hurts, giving it another go; and I alongside them.

Or is it closer still than that? Has Ella outlived her past this time around? Does she see her ancient self-wrestling with the old pain here now in the body of a great niece who finally heard her? Or was it James who was the one who haunted me? Was his story the one most in need of telling? Or Mary's?

Have they all come back to resolve to save future generations from the fateful inheritance?

> *When you understood the great round, then you could change things, even after they happened, because every chance came again, if you recognized it.*

> – Elizabeth Cunningham

EPILOGUE

Following the writing of this book, I read *'This Rash Act': Suicide Across the Life Cycle in the Victorian City* by Victor Bailey. I was affirmed by what I discovered there. Though he bases his research on the midlands of England in the late nineteenth century, the motivations, the reaction of the culture of the time, the place of the coroner and juries, and the reporting all resonated with what I discovered in the story of the Condon family of Iowa.

Here are some of the interesting things Mr. Bailey uncovered in his research:

Coroners as we know them today are doctors. That was not necessarily so in the nineteenth century, for back then they may have been lawyers or law officials.

Suicides for the most part were consigned to two causes, organic (from the individual) and societal. The motives may have been an event, extremes of loneliness and isolation, societal changes as industry followed close on the heels of pastoral life, poverty, physical and mental illness, romantic disappointment, conflict between parents and children, spouses, old age, alcoholism, severance from family, friends or neighborhood, out of wedlock pregnancy, unemployment, an overwhelming sense of being unable to deal with anymore disappointment or loss, even religious zealotry with its emphasis on sin, guilt and shame.

Domestic service was a lonely, demanding and never-ending occupation. In such surroundings, depression, romantic disappointment and employer admonishment could take on exaggerated dimensions. In all, domestic service provided one of the most crucial settings for the suicide of young adult women.

Far and away the most important determination of young female suicides was disturbance in personal relationships (bereavement, romantic disappointment, family quarrels). This includes illegitimate pregnancy.

Recording Suicides:

The recording of suicide is said to be complicated by two major sources of systematic reporting error:

1. Concealment of suicides, notably by social groups such as Catholics and families of higher social standing, who, like Mr. Power in James Joyce's *Ulysses,* looked upon suicide as "the greatest disgrace to have in the family." It is often claimed, too, that families, tried in particular to conceal female suicides.
2. The second source of error is said to be misclassification of deaths by coroners, who differed in their qualifications to judge the cause of death and on the resources available to conduct their investigations.

Nor can newspaper accounts of inquest proceedings be relied upon. Press reporting was selective, inclining to the unusual methods and motives, and it embodied, not to say, molded contemporary perceptions of suicide . . . The glimpses of life and death in depositions, are, said Radcliffe, 'shadows that are more projections of observers views and phantasms than the reality of self destruction. The assigned motive, that proffered by coroner or witness, is merely the folk explanation of suicide. The true motive (what was in the suicide's mind) is impenetrable.

Major Factors:

"In all cases, the feeling of a relentless and irremediable solitude is the 'unique cause of all suicide.'" (Maurice Halbwachs, *The Causes of Suicide,* 1930, quoted in *'This Rash Act')*

The fact that self-destruction is always preventable, and that family members often had a role in the causal process leading to the suicide, could well have influenced the way that witnesses reconstructed the past. It is unrealistic to expect witnesses to admit readily to deep-seated family tensions, say, when such an admission might deflect badly upon themselves or other survivors.

"Spare a suicide's family the social disgrace of a clandestine, non-Christian burial." This was often the motivation in the reporting of "accidental deaths."

In my research through the Black Hawk County Death Records, I came upon countless numbers of infant deaths, accidents, and unknown causes. I could not help but wonder how many were infanticide, suicide, or homicide. During the nineteenth century, one almost had to be present and watch the person commit suicide, collect a suicide note, and speak to the despondency of the person in order for it to be recorded as such. We have come a long way since then.

ACKNOWLEDGMENTS

Grout Genealogical Library, Grout Museum, Waterloo, Iowa
Waterloo Public Library Microfiche Archive
Waterloo Daily Courier
Black Hawk County Recorder's Office

'This Rash Act': Suicides Across the Life Cycle in the Victorian City by Victor Bailey
Stanford University Press, 1998
Waterloo Cedar Falls, A Pictorial History, Margaret Corwin and Helen Hoy
Selected Poems & Letters of Emily Dickinson, edited by Robert Linscott, Anchor Books,
    Doubleday, 1959
W. B. Yeats, Selected Poems, Gramercy Books, 1992
Great Love Poems, edited by Shane Weller, Dover Publications, Inc., 1992

Donna Condon, who helped with the research
Patrick Hennessey, who encouraged my writing
Glenn Ambrose, who provided the space
The Condon Family of Waterloo, Iowa

Picture #16 – (Judith Condon, Author)

Judith Condon, born in 1949 in Waterloo, Iowa, has spent her life involved in several endeavors from teacher to chaplain and social services to mother, grandmother, writer, and keeper of the family stories. She currently resides in Minneapolis, Minnesota.

INDEX

www.ingramcontent.com/pod-product-compliance
Lightning Source LLC
Chambersburg PA
CBHW021228280526
45784CB00005B/2017